Seymour Dexter, Union Army

Seymour Dexter, Union Army

*Journal and Letters of Civil War Service
in Company K, 23rd New York Volunteer
Regiment of Elmira, with Illustrations*

edited by
CARL A. MORRELL

McFarland & Company, Inc., Publishers
Jefferson, North Carolina, and London

Frontispiece: Ellenoir Dexter and Seymour Dexter (photographs from collection of Carl Morrell)

British Library Cataloguing-in-Publication data are available

Library of Congress Cataloguing-in-Publication Data

Dexter, Seymour, 1841–1904.
    Seymour Dexter, Union Army : journal and letters of civil war service in Company K, 23rd New York Volunteer Regiment of Elmira, with illustrations / edited by Carl A. Morrell.
       p.   cm.
    Includes bibliographical references (p.) and index.
    ISBN 0-7864-0197-4 (library binding : 55# alk. paper) ∞
    1. Dexter, Seymour, 1841–1904—Diaries. 2. Dexter, Seymour, 1841–1904—Correspondence. 3. United States. Army. New York Infantry Regiment, 23rd (1861–1865). Company K—Biography. 4. Soldiers—New York (State)—Diaries. 5. Soldiers—New York (State)—Correspondence. 6. New York (State)—History—Civil War, 1861–1865—Personal narratives. 7. United States—History—Civil War, 1861–1865—Personal narratives. 8. Elmira (N.Y.)—Biography. I. Morrell, Carl A., 1916– . II. Title.
E523.5 23rd.D49   1996
973.7'8147—dc20   96-33265
                                                          CIP

Manufactured in the United States of America

McFarland & Company, Inc., Publishers
  Box 611, Jefferson, North Carolina 28640

This book is
respectfully dedicated to the
unsung foot soldiers of the
Civil War

Contents

List of Illustrations
and Maps

MAPS

Preface

Seymour Dexter's letters to his school sweetheart cover the time of enlistment in Elmira when he was mustered into the 23rd with his companions from Alfred, until late 1864. He was mustered out of the army in May 1863 after his two years were up, but a few letters are carried on into late 1864, at which time he was a law apprentice in the offices of Woods & Turner.

"The Journal of 1861" which has become part of the story of Company K covers a period only from the time that Seymour and his friends heeded Abraham Lincoln's April call for men to serve until the close of 1861. The journal aptly covered most of Company K's travels.

The letters to Ellie (Ellenoir) start before the journal writings, although I am using the first part of the journal because of its nature as an introduction. The letters follow. From there on as the story unfolds, the journal will take over. The first few letters and the journal run approximately the same, but I have omitted parts that I felt were not necessary nor pertinent to the story of Company K. To support the facts in the letters to Ellie I have added battle reports by his superior officers to augment Seymour's own personal military and political feelings. The reader must bear in mind that the letters and journal transcriptions are unabridged; any errors in spelling or grammar have been left as written. My own commentary, which is intended to provide background and introduce certain letters and texts from sources other than Dexter's, is in italics.

Seymour's writing of the journal from May 1861 until the close of 1861 was written with no concern for paragraphing nor dating. I have paragraphed where I felt that it was needed.

—C.A.M.

1

Introduction

On September 1, 1830, the New York State militia authorized a unit to be formed. Under the leadership of Captain Joseph Hoffman, a unit was activated that called itself the Elmira Guards. The Elmira Guards remained in active duty to the state, participating in active drills, camp outs, maneuvers and rifle practice. In 1854 the Elmira Guards disbanded and reformed as the Southern Tier Rifles. Captain Henry C. Hoffman became the commanding officer of the newly named unit.

At that time, the Rifles entered into more vigorous activity than ever with very rigid physical and moral standards for its members. They drilled laboriously and maintained strict discipline. Uniforms were at all times neatly shaped and shoes polished. All men were required to attend all organizational activities in full uniform. Excess absenteeism and drunkenness could be cause for expulsion.

The Guard met twice a week for drill and the men were required to buy their own uniforms, muskets and equipment. Just prior to the outbreak of the Civil War, the State of New York began a policy of uniform and equipment purchases. The Southern Tier Rifles were justly proud of their organization.

At the outbreak of the Civil War there were 65 men, three commissioned officers and one non-commissioned officer in the Rifles. It was this group that became the nucleus of the 23rd Regiment.

Volunteers poured into Elmira from all parts of the Southern Tier and as the regiment grew the camps in Elmira swelled with manpower. At long last the regiment was in full complement with men from all walks of life from Elmira and the surrounding area.

The regiment consisted of 10 companies from Steuben, Alleghany, Tioga, Schuyler, Cortland and Chemung counties. The 23rd, after a period of training, left Elmira for Washington, D. C., on July 5, 1861, with 781 men.

The saga of Company K, 23rd N.Y. Volunteer from Elmira, N.Y., is probably no different, no more nor less glorious than any other division, regiment or company that either was drafted or volunteered to serve time in the 1860s. It is filled with heartbreak, tragedy and humor.

The men of Company K marched no one knows how many miles in stifling heat, in drenching rains that made mud sloughs of the pikes, and in bitter cold with snow and sleet that chilled one to the bone. They knew the loneliness of continual picket duty on a desolate outpost in a strange country far from camp.

For Company K, the fortunes of war did not weigh too heavily in terms of casualties. Eighteen men were killed in action, 32 died from disease and 16 were taken prisoner.

It is notable that of the 16 men taken prisoner 10 were captured at the second battle of Bull Run. By August 1863, all 16 men had been paroled by the Confederates and 15 of them rejoined the 23rd for active duty.

Timeline of
Seymour Dexter's Life

1841   Born March 20 at Independence, N.Y., son of Daniel Dexter and Angeline Briggs.

1860   Attended Alfred Academy, Wellsville, N.Y.

1861   Attended Alfred University and then enlisted as a private in Company K, 23rd N.Y. Volunteer at the time of the firing on Fort Sumter. After two years returned to the University.

1864   Graduated from Alfred University—moved to Elmira, N.Y., pursued his legal studies and was admitted to the bar.

1866   Became a law partner of Robert T. Turner.

1868   Joined the law firm of Turner, Dexter & Van Duzen.

1872   Appointed city attorney and elected member of the Assembly of Albany, N.Y. (first Republican elected from Chemung County in sixteen years).

1878   Elected county judge.

1885   Resigned judgeship to be president of Second National Bank.

1885   Received a Ph.D. from Alfred University.

1889   Wrote first publication that set forth the advantages of Savings and Loan—"Treatise on Cooperative Savings."

1890   Founder and president of N.Y. State League of Cooperative Savings & Loan.

1903   LL.D. from Alfred University.

1904   Died May 5.

Other Accomplishments and Memberships

- Founder and president of Chemung Valley Savings and Loan Association.
- Trustee of Alfred University.
- Treasurer and member of board of Elmira College.
- Member of Board and a vice president of N.Y. State Reformatory in Elmira, N.Y. (conducted classes in political economy for the inmates while a member of the board).
- Member of New York Chamber of Commerce.
- Active member of Park Church and close friend of Thomas K. Beecher (whose half-sister was Harriet Beecher Stowe).
- Friend of Samuel L. Clemens (Mark Twain).
- President of the Elmira Advertising Association.
- Married Ellenoir Weaver (also a graduate of Alfred University). They had six children: Eleanor, Daniel, Adelaide, Mary, Luin, Emily.

The First of
the Journal Writings

Journal 1861

There are times in the history of every nation when the foundation of its existence has been shaken to its very center, either by an external invasion or internal disruption. In a crisis to the latter character our own beloved country has become involved, at present. The antagonistical elements, freedom and slavery which have been so long warring against each other have assumed a more belligerent position. Slavery having lost its supremacy in the ballot box, it has attempted to attain its end by the power of arms. It has bid defiance to the legal constituted authorities, seized our revenue and stolen our property, beseiged and taken our forts, hurled down the stars and stripes and in their place hoisted a flag emblematical of the diabolical system which it nourishes and now it has assembled a vast army and threatens to destroy or siege the capitol of the nation and has even boasted that it would raise the secession flag upon Bunker Hill's Monument.

Freedom, the true government has called upon her loyal sons to flock to her standard and defend her honor and maintain her supremacy, it must be, on the field of battle.

Our response to this call and also to the demands of truth and humanity, seven of us classmates and students at Alfred Academy (L.K. THATCHER, W.W. BROWN, C.A. CHAPIN, L. KENYON, L.L. BACON, J.C. TODD and myself) determined on the 26th day of April, 1861 that we would immediately volunteer our services in the defense of the stars and stripes. In accordance with this determination we immediately laid aside our books which had been our constant companions for many terms and prepared to depart in the morning for some place of enlistment. As soon as it was reported about town that we were going, friends came around us inquiring if it was really the

77.53.1

Seymour Dexter.
23rd Regiment N.Y. Vol.
Co. K. Arlington Heights Va.
Aug. 10th 1861.

Frontispiece of Seymour Dexter's journal.

case. Upon being answered in the affirmative they would speak words of encouragement and also express a desire to aid us in every way that was in their power. The afternoon and evening were spent in making preparations for our departure in the morning.

The morning broke beautifully bright and clear. When it had become known that we were going for a certainty three more of our classmates resolved that they would go with us (T.C. SANDERS, M. SHEPPERED AND A. SEARS). We took breakfast at the Holland where we passed many a joke. After we had finished our meal we immediately went to the Chapel. Here a scene transpired which will ever remain fresh in my memory. Here the depths of that friendship which existed between student and student, student and teacher was plainly shown by the emotions depicted upon the countenance of everyone present.

Many citizens were also present all of whom participated in the same feeling. They raised Fifty dollars to pay our expenses and buy necessary comforts. The teachers all made short speeches and then it fell to our lot to make a few farewell remarks. We did not get away from Chapel until nearly 10 o'clock and teams were in readiness to take us to Hornellsville. As we proceeded to take our seats in the wagons the last scene transpired, that of shaking hands and saying farewell. Often have I parted with friends before but never under circumstances so peculiar, so fitted to call forth the true sentiment of the heart. But the last word was spoken and away we rode, bound for Hornellsville. It was our determination either to enlist at this place or proceed to Elmira, to which place three of our friends had gone upon the 22nd according as we could best suit ourselves. We arrived at Hornellsville a little after noon and proceeded to the home of Mr. Thatcher where we partook of an excellent dinner.

After dinner was over we walked down to the drill room of the company that was then forming at this place. Lt. Col. Crane of the 60th State Militia Regt., was then drilling a squad of new volunteers. It was our desire to enlist in a company possessing as good morals and as much intelligence as we could find. Thinking that we saw far different qualities manifested in this company we determined to try and see what could be done at Elmira. Proceeding to the office we telegraphed to one of our friends (Williams) inquiring what would be our chance to enlist in the same company with them (The Southern Tier Rifles of Elmira) then reported as the best company in southern N.Y. We soon received a dispatch simply saying to us to come on. But in a short time we received another from the Capt. of the company (H.C. Hoffman) stating that we could not do better than to come on to Elmira. Taking a vote we decided to go. Starting in the morning at 7:56 through the hospitality of Mr. Thatcher's people we were well provided for during our tarry. To them we owe a debt of gratitude to be repaid by ever standing firm by the stars and stripes.

Eight o'clock in the morning found us seated upon the express bound for Elmira. As we swept down the Canisteo Valley, beautiful in the morning sun, many were the thoughts that passed through our minds. Most of us had come without seeing our parents or any of our friends at home. We arrived at the point of our destination a little after ten o'clock and immediately proceeded to the Brainard House where we took dinner. We soon found the other boys (Williams and the two Maxsons) who said the company was full but they said the best thing would be done for us that could be. After taking dinner we repaired to the drill room, we were well suited to their appearance and by the interposition and recommendation of friends succeeded in being admitted to the company that evening. We thought that we had been extremely fortunate whether we were or not has yet to be revealed in the future. We had learned at least that all is not gold that glitters. A fund had been raised by the city to pay the expenses of volunteers while drilling. Hence, as soon as we became members of the company they had to provide us with a boarding place. They sent us to the Haights Hotel where we had rooms and every convenience the same as travelers. We remained here until the company was mustered into the state service and began to draw rations from the state which was about two weeks afterwards.

Barracks Number 6

Seymour is anxious for words from his classmates at Alfred although it has only been a few days since they had left the Academy.

Elmira Haights Hotel
Elmira, N. Y.
May 3, 1861
Sunday Morning

My Dear Friend:

I have never wanted half so bad in the world to hear from my friends and family as I have this morning. I presume that Williams has given you a description of our drilling. You wanted to know how I liked drilling on Sunday? Well, to be frank, I do not like it very well, but I cast a soothing balm upon my conscience by thinking that I am preparing myself to defend the cause of truth, humanity, and justice. I presume from what I have told you, you know that I do not believe that religion consists in laying aside work from sunset to sunset, or from midnite to midnite, but that it consists in the contrition of the heart, for it is the heart that motivates that influence, that God judges.

The day before yesterday I visited Mr. Sinnett's Picture Gallery for the purpose of viewing the noted German painting "Holy Night," which is on exhibition there. It is one of the most beautiful things I ever saw.

The Beecher's rooms (the Congregational Church) are always open to us at any time for prayer meetings. It may surprise you to know that I attended a prayer meeting Wednesday evening.

I have seen more drunkedness and swearing since I left Alfred than I have seen or heard in all my life. Luin K. Thatcher, Wallace Brown and myself went up to the barracks last night after supper. You cannot imagine the degradation that seems to be indelibly stamped upon at least one half of the soldiers. A regiment from Syracuse numbering 810 came in last night making in all now in Elmira about 1600, I should judge. As regards to leaving we have no idea when it will be. The inhabitants want this one to stay here for they are afraid of riot, because they are getting so many rough soldiers in and about the place.

Last evening there must have been 200 ladies in the drill room as spectators. When our time was about half gone the alarm of fire made a scattering among the audience.

If there is anything I stand in need of I will let you know.

Seymour

Water St., Elmira, NY
Dr. Grezo's
May 9, 1861

My Dear Friend:

As you perceive, I have changed quarters. We were mustered into the state service yesterday and according to the rolls we should have moved into barracks and have drawn regular army rations but Capt. Hoffman knew that we did not want to do that, so he took the contract of feeding us and he gave us the privilege of drawing the money for our board (which is .45 per day) and using it where we had a mind to go and, of course, we accepted that chance.

We came (Wallace Brown and Tommy Sanders) down here to Dr. Grezo's who is his uncle and procured a place for the four of us. The other boys are in different places.

Elmira is full of soldiers, there is now between 4,000 and 5,000 and they are coming in all the time. Taking them altogether they are the heartiest soldiers I ever saw. From all accounts yesterday it is altogether probable that a portion of the troops here will be called away very soon, but we can not tell.

Time for mail call... Seymour

Robert V. Valkenberg, original colonel of the 107th New York Volunteer, wearing the uniform of a brigadier general, New York State Militia (courtesy Chemung County Historical Society).

Elmira, NY
May 15, 1861

Dear Ellie;

I have just returned from drill. It is a little after five o'clock. We have been traveling most of the time since 2 o'clock. We have been out of town over some two miles to a cemetery. It is a new cemetery for the city and contains over 60 acres of land. It is situated on a rising piece of ground from which there is one of the finest landscape views I have ever seen.

From there we came past the female college which seems to delight the company because it torments the principal of the college. The boys say that the principal of the school has been to Gen. Van Valkenberg and wished to forbid the soldiers from drilling in that part of the city because it draws the attention of his girls, as is apt to be the case—the girls are not to blame, it's human nature.

The company formed here in Elmira together with the ones from Hornellsville, Bath and Corning and three from Binghamton together with two others to make out ten companies that have been organized into a regiment today. They have elected Capt. Hoffman a commander so we will have him for a Captain.

Half past ten in the evening and I have just returned from a serenading march. Our company headed by the Elmira Cornet Band left headquarters at 8 p.m. and proceeded to Capt. Hoffman's which is nearly a mile distant (528 W. Water St.) for the purpose of serenading and congratulating him upon his promotion. When we arrived there he invited the company in and treated them with whisky, wine and cigars. I think that everyone in the company drank except the Alfred boys. From Capt. Hoffman's we proceeded to Major Greggs who was a second Lt. in our company and was promoted to Major in the regiment. (17 Sullivan St. Cor. Sullivan & E. Second St.) Here the same thing took place again, with the exception that the boys drank a good deal more. By the time we got back to the barracks it started to rain and with all I am fatigued more than any night that I have been here.

Elmira now has almost as many soldiers as it has inhabitants. The number is somewhere between 8,000–9,000, but there is better order than has been. I am fearful that we shall be moving into barracks, although we do enjoy ourselves at Dr. Grezo's.

If I am here after the fourth of July, I will be up to Alfred, if I can get away before we go south.

Seymour

Elmira, NY
Dr. Grezo's
May 25, 1861

Dear Ellie:

We have been much pleased with telegraph dispatch which came through this forenoon, regarding the battle of Sewell's Point. The killing of between 3,000–4,000 rebels and their complete defeat. If the report is true I think that northern "Mud Sills" can fight. The death of Col. Ellsworth was recognized here yesterday by the flags being lowered to half mast. (A hotel keeper shot Col. Ellsworth in Alexandria while coming down a stairway in the Alexandria Hotel after lowering a confederate flag.)

The officers for the regiment have not yet been appointed by Governor Morgan. All the officers must enlist for three years.

Seymour

Seymour has now been gone from home over three weeks and like any young man, misses home, friends, and more than ever looks for mail from home even though he is with some of his buddies from Alfred.

The battle at Sewell's Point was highly exaggerated in reference to the number killed. Actually, no casualties were reported. According to a Confederate report, the U.S.S. Monticello opened fire upon the unfinished batteries at Sewell's Point on May 18, 1861. Gen. Gwynn hurried five pieces of artillery down from Norfolk, placed them in position and returned fire on the 19th; the firing disabled the U.S.S. Monticello and she withdrew.

Elmira, NY
Barracks #6
June 6, 1861

Dear Ellie:

We are now in our new barracks. Our barrack is about 60 feet long by 16 feet wide, and made out of rough boards. Our bunks are arranged along the sides two deep. (One above the other). A tick filled with straw and a blanket constitutes the bedding of each soldier. It will suffice for the warm weather. The cooking establishment and dining hall is directly back of the barrack and are now cooking for 750 men.

The training grounds now have a complete guard staff of soldiers (officers of the guard) on duty around the clock. Nobody in and nobody out without a pass.

I have enjoyed the routine, we get up at 5 a.m. and roll call at 5:30. Breakfast a short while after six then we drill under respective captains and drill until around 11 or 11:30 a.m. Dinner is at twelve and then regimental drill from half past one until half past four. Supper at six and parade at seven. Then the regiment is drawn up on the line and general orders are given. We generally retire at 10 p.m.

Commander Van Valkenberg has clamped down on passes. No more than three men can leave the grounds at one time and no more than six per day.

Seymour

The meals so far have been very plain. Seymour makes several references in his letters to plain meat and potatoes, bean soup, no butter, even mush and milk. Most of the men complained bitterly about the food being so badly cooked.

Elmira, NY
Barracks #6
June 14, 1861

Dear Friend Eleanor:

Our company is the only real company that has been on drill this forenoon. There is much dissatisfaction among most of the companies that the officers are afraid to call them out to drill, fearing that they will refuse to drill and go home en mass. The dissatisfaction is caused principly by the delay which exists in the regiment receiving their uniforms and pay which should have been received before this.

Seymour

Seymour Dexter (courtesy Alfred University Library).

Seymour now confesses that he would rather be home with Ellie and his friends than in camp among the men. Profanity is rampant and drunkenness a common vice among the ranks. He expects a furlough next week and is anxiously looking forward to a few days at home.

Journal
After June 14, 1861

    Amid the various changes and scenes through which we had passed since we became soldiers, often in spirit we had left our present

Four of the 17 soldiers in Company K, 23rd Regiment, from Alfred University. From left: Wallace Brown, William Maxson, Luin Thatcher, and Seymour Dexter. Note wood frame with tent overlay (courtesy of Chemung County Historical Society).

surroundings and scenes of the past seemed to be lived over again in sweet reverie. Would home with its dearest friends, its hallowed association and elevating influences sweep before the minds eye. At one time unrolled from memories sacred scroll, at another the present would be sketched in brilliant colors by imagination's artistic hand.

School day scenes and associations and attachments formed sweetened many an hour of calm meditation thought by their ever pleasant rememberances.

As the time for the separation of the band of students was at hand with whom we had been so long joined by school association and influences and there was no prospect of leaving Elmira in the next two or three weeks, we determined, if possible, to get a furlough and visit our homes and attend the anniversary of the school, which was upon the 26th. Accordingly during the afternoon we were sworn in we succeeded in getting a furlough until the next Thursday morning.

Barracks #6 (after June 14, 1861)

Picking up things that we wished to take home, we took an evening train for Alfred where we arrived at 1 o'clock in the a.m. Chapin and Kenyon did not stop but proceeded directly to their home. Thatcher also stopped at his home. Williams went and stayed at a sister's near Alfred Station. The rest of us walked up to the Center where we arrived about 2 o'clock a.m. Brown (my old chum) and myself went to our old room and laid ourselves down to rest. It was my intention to have went home that night, but the cars would not stop for me. Accordingly the next morning after taking breakfast at the Hall where I met many of my classmates I hired a horse and buggy and immediately started for home. Half past twelve found me once more sitting beneath the parental roof. I had almost feared that my visit would be saddened by the fact that I was at home for the last time altogether probably before we started for the soil of the "Old Dominion."

I had promised to return to Alfred at noon upon the next day. About nine a.m. I hitched my horse and prepared to return. I did not have time to bid my parents and sisters goodbye since they were coming out to Alfred upon the following Wednesday. As I seated myself on the carriage father came up and I was about to bid him good morning when he remarked, "Seymour take a good look at the scene around you. This may be the last time you will ever look upon the hills of your

Alfred Academy—founded in 1836. This building still stands on the Alfred University Campus next to the Herrick Library (courtesy Alfred University Library).

birthplace." Those words seemed to touch my heart, the scene was beautiful in the morning sun. Whether I shall ever be permitted to look upon those dearly loved hills is locked up in the bosom of HIM who "knoweth all things."

I arrived at Alfred where I spent nearly three days as agreeable as I ever spent the same length of time in my life. It was spent in visiting and attending the sessions of the literary societies. Tuesday evening, we attended the Rev. Chapin upon "Man and his works." It was a sublime production and delivered in an oratory peculiar to Chapin. Wednesday was anniversary day. The institution confered the degree upon those of us who were to have graduated the same as though we had received the full term. That afternoon is one long to be held fresh on memories pages, as long as life is spared. I shall always remember the anguish on my mother's heart, the deep concealed grief of my father, the unrestrained emotions of my sisters as I impressed the kiss and said the last farewell. It seems like a dream to think that I am separated from them by such a distance and by such circumstances as I am at present.

The alumni of the institution met at five o'clock. We had an interesting time and until seven when we repaired to the supper table. After partaking of a bountiful repast before us nearly three hours was spent in speaking. A great many of the old graduates who had returned to make a short visit to the scene of their old schooldays. They all spoke words of encouragement and advice to the new class. After this came the scene of bidding our classmates the last farewell. We were to be separated in every direction and under all probability never all meet together again. I will not attempt to describe the emotions of the heart in such a parting and one so peculiar as the present. The last farewell was spoken and at last we retired for the night. Four o'clock in the morning found us gayly driving along towards Hornellsville, where we were to take an express for Elmira. Half past nine found us back in the barracks with little sleep which we earnestly desired but back on duty. Not until now did I little realize that I had parted with my friends for at least two years and perhaps forever upon earth. As I thought upon it in my heart "Shall I ever see their faces." The future is uncertain and I answered back "God only Knows."

Elmira Barracks #6
June 30, 1861

Dear Ellie:

It is Sunday morning and the church bells are just beginning to ring as I commence writing. It is a beautiful morning, the sound of the

church bells sends scenes of the past thronging before my minds eye upon memories wing, Sundays spent under so different circumstances from those of today.

I am a dishwasher today, it is my first experience & I thank my stars that I have not got to follow it for life. Brown & Bacon are my companions in the business today. We made up our minds this morning that if the knives & forks were left a little greasy they would not rust. On account of this dish washing I shall have to stay at the barracks today, but it will be the means of giving you a good long letter.

When we got back the other morning we found the barracks almost deserted, there were so many home on furloughs. We got into the grounds without any trouble. We came up and put on a good face and went to talking with the sergeant of the guard for a few moments and he let us in without wanting to see our furlough which had run out the day before.

We had battalion drill in the afternoon and also in the evening. I came near getting to sleep in the ranks while we were resting. We all came on guard Friday but we had about caught up in sleeping by Friday night. No doubt you slept well that night. Yesterday afternoon or rather near supper time we had a strawberry feast. Alexander Diven M.C. and Hall, a partner of his in business, had extended an invitation to our company and the other Elmira companies and field officers of the regiment to meet at Hall's home yesterday afternoon to eat strawberries and ice cream. Our martial band gave us the music and they gave us all the strawberries, ice cream and milk that we could dispose of.

The report was that orders to leave had come in while we were on furlough last Friday but not being prepared our departure has been put off until the 4th or 6th which of these days is not yet fully determined. We shall leave on the fourth if things can be made ready. One week from today I expect to be in Washington or on the way there.

We have all gear except our camp equipment, which I presume we shall not receive until we arrive in Washington or Harper's Ferry.

C.A. Chapin is sick with the measles, he was just coming down with them at Alfred. The next morning he was all spotted. I am fearful that he will not be well enough to go when we go. He is now at a private house downtown where he will have good care taken of him.

Luin is downtown today, I presume he is visiting with Skip Howell. Luin & myself had photographs taken Friday afternoon with our

Opposite: *Elmira Cornet Band (courtesy Library of Congress).*

soldiers rig on, revolver and gun. We could not get them until tomorrow. I will send you mine either in this letter or the next one I write.

I just begin to fully realize that I am not again to meet the faces of dear friends for a long time and perhaps never. That word never grates harshly upon the heart. Can it be so? I trust in God that it is not. I want to meet my parents and sisters again. I want to meet thee again. When true friends are separated from each other and that too by such circumstances as separate me from my friends at present affection for them burns stronger.

The heart according to the laws of its own action, points out those whom it truly loves. The probability is that we shall leave here next Thursday. I should like to hear from you before we go, or as soon as we arrive at our point of destination.

Direct your letters to

> Seymour Dexter
> 23rd. Regiment N.Y. Volunteers
> Care of Capt. W.B. Fowler
> Elmira

P.S. Directed thus it will follow us wherever we are. Will you? Ellie remember me in your evening meditations. Will you remember me ever as a true and dear friend.

Seymour Dexter

The following letter was posted prior to the departure to Washington, D.C., July 5th, 1861. The letter was franked by Alexander Diven who at the time was a member of Congress and later to become a colonel in the 107th Infantry under Col. Robert B. Van Valkenberg. The envelope was overweight because of photographs that were being sent to Ellie, thus postage due. The letter was backstamped in oval with "DEAD LETTER OFFICE PO DEPT. POSTAGE NOT PAID," and backstamped July 19th, 1861, Elmira, N.Y. The front of the envelope was franked and marked held for postage and stamped "DUE 6 cts."

Envelope (front and back) of Seymour's July 3, 1861, letter to Ellenoir.

Elmira Barracks #6
July 3rd 1861

Dear Ellie,

I take up my pen to drop you a short note with the pictures which you find enclosed. A lot of Alfred folks are here at present, Mrs. Prof. Allen, Mrs. Taylor, Mr. Coon and Addie Chadwick, they came down Monday afternoon and are not going home until tomorrow morning. I wish you had been with them. I believe Prof. Allen goes home on the express this evening.

It is now Wednesday morning, the fourth of July, and what a beautiful morning it is. Our departure from here has been postponed until tomorrow morning at nine o'clock. We are to have everything in readiness tonight. The Ladies of Elmira will treat us to a splendid supper tonight at 5 p.m. C.H. Chapin is not well enough to go with us. He feels very sorry about it.

We all went down to the Delevan House last night and had a fine visit with the Alfred Girls. Thatcher wished that there were two or three other girls there that he knew. I seconded his wish.

This is my last letter to you from Elmira. If you should not hear from me so often hereafter you must lay it on to the mail arrangements and not from my negligence in writing. So farewell to you, Dear Friend, from Elmira barracks #6.

Your true friend & admirer
S Dexter

Drills, Picket Duty
and Marches:
July–December 1861

*Letter postmarked Washington, July 10, 1861, free franked by
David Wilmot, member of Congress. David Wilmot was the
sponsor of the Wilmot Proviso.*

Meridian Hill, Washington
July 8, 1861

Dear Ellie:

I am seated in the shade formed by the boughs. Some 700 men
are seated around us in the woods lying in the shade. We came up here
this morning from the City of Washington at a distance of 2-1/2 miles.
We left the city at 9 a.m. marching up Pennsylvania Ave. We passed
the Patent Office building which is a magnificent structure built of
marble. It is one of the warmest days of the season and a great number of our regiment sunk down by the road overcome by the heat. As
for myself, I think I was never warmer in my life but did not feel
exhausted in the least. When we reached the grounds we all made a
rush for the woods where we stayed until we cooled off.

We left Elmira last Friday at half past eleven in the morning.
There was one of the greatest crowds out to witness our departure I
ever saw. Many were the hearts that were stirred to their deepest foun-
tains with emotions of sorrow caused by parting with husbands, brothers, sons and lovers. As we steamed away cheer after cheer went up
from the vast multitude for the Southern Tier Regiment. The first
place that we made a halt, except for wood and water, was Williamsport

where the ladies had prepared a bounteous dinner for us. We arrived there a little after 3 o'clock and left about 5 o'clock p.m. The scenery from there to Maryland line is beautiful. Much better than I had expected to see. We passed Harrisburg in the night hence we did not see it at all. We arrived at Baltimore the next day at 10:30 a.m. We unloaded from the cars and formed a line of battle then wheeled into column and marched through the city with our colors flying and band playing. No insults were offered us but, on the other hand, the red, white and blue was shown from most every house upon the street. We had good passenger cars until we arrived here, but from here we went to Washington in freight cars with rough boards in for seats. We passed the relay house and Annapolis junction in going from Baltimore to Washington.

We waited at the latter place from a little after 1 p.m. until dark for trains to pass. When we arrived at Washington there was so much baggage that we could not get to the depot with the train so we had to get off the train a little ways out of town. It was very dark and we had something of a sweet time getting into the city, I reckon. When we did get in they undertook to quarter us in the basement of a church but it was so filthy that we would not stay there, but rather sleep on the sidewalk which we have done for two nights in succession. It was 2 o'clock when I laid down to sleep upon the soft side of a board. When we left Elmira we took three days rations in our haversacks, that got pretty mussed up by the time we made Washington. So. I had to get by with what I had to eat except some sea crackers. Nobody has anything to eat yet today. Our quartermaster had better come around with provisions before long or there will be a mutiny in the camp.

Tues. a.m., cont.

I was interrupted yesterday in writing this letter by our camps coming. We had to lay aside all else and pitch tents. We have at last commenced soldier's life in true earnest. We have to do our own cooking. I won't say anything about the coffee, or how we got up for breakfast this morning. I had to grind the coffee with a stone in an iron dish and the rice burned upon the bottom of the kettle.

I do not think that we will be here very long. I think we shall be on Virginia soil by the time two weeks have passed. There has been fighting so near that we could hear the cannon. One of the boys was talking to Senator Sumner and he remarked that there would be a big battle before next Sunday. Ten regiments have left the city since yesterday for the scene of action. All the land around Washington seems almost like a vast tented field the camps are so thick.

Your true friend,
Seymour

Envelope mailed from Washington. Free franked by Congressman N.A. Harris, dated July 16, 1861.

Meridian Heights
Camp Diven
July 15, 1861

Dear Ellie:

It is Monday afternoon. I was on guard last night and have been sleeping all the forenoon. Awakened just as mail call came in and there was no letter for me. I was not disappointed for I hardly expected one. I then took my writing materials and came down into the woods where I am now, beyond the turmoil of the camp, to have an easy talk with you.

When I wrote before to you we had just settled upon our present camping ground, since that time we have been living in true soldier style. We have our full amount of tents now and there are five of us together in a tent.

Brown, Thatcher, Bacon, Sanders and myself are together. There is not much chance to get lonesome when we are all there. We live in grand style. Our house is about 8 feet square upon the bottom, running to a peak at the top. For convenience we have our parlor, sitting room and bed room all together. Our bedstead is a pine board laid upon the ground, the bedding is an India rubber blanket and a bed tick to lay upon the board and a blanket to spread over us. Our pillow is our knapsack with our coat and something similar to throw upon it. As for eating, as some of the boys say, that is "played out." Our company have hired cooks so we do not have to do our own cooking any longer. We have two meals a day. For the first meal, with two exceptions, we have coffee with but little sugar and no milk in it and the fattest kind of pork and poor bread. For the other meal sometimes we would have the same fare and at others we have some rice. The two other exceptions I speak of is when we have fresh beef. I have not eaten as much in two days as I would have eaten in one meal at home, and since the cooking for the whole company has been done altogether if one is not on time he will not get anything. Perhaps if I keep on in this way much longer you will think I am sick of soldiering. No. I am here while my country needs my service. When I can get enough to eat I enjoy myself here first rate.

I have spent two days since we came up here in the city. Last Wednesday Bacon and myself got a pass in the morning and went to the Treasury building which is an immense building of marble. From there we went to the White House, the residence of Old Abe, going in the front door we passed through a hall into his reception room or what is known in print as the East Room. It is a magnificent sight. It is the room that the president holds his levees. We also went into what is called the Green Room and then went out and viewed the grounds around the house, these are beautifully decorated. From there we went down to the Potomac past Washington's monument and then back to the Patent Office, took refreshments at a saloon and then spent about an hour and a half in passing a portion of this building. In that time one cannot view one-hundredth part of the models and relics that are here. Perhaps one of the most sacred relics to be seen here is the sword of Washington and the dress he wore when he resigned his commission to Congress. From the Patent Office we went to the Capitol and first went into the Senate. Language fails to describe the beauty there is about this building, both inside and outside. It is truly a feast to sit in those galleries surrounded by such magnificence as you are, and at the same time feel you are in the presence of the Statesmen of the nation.

After staying here a while we went into the House of Representatives but they had adjourned so we spent the afternoon in the Senate. We heard some 8 or 9 different ones make short speeches but what pleased me most of all was to meet Prof. Allen, from Alfred University, in the gallery. He came up to our camp yesterday and stayed with us. Last Friday we went to the city and visited the Smithsonian Institute. This time one of the great curiosities that I saw here was an Egyptian mummy. One can look at the curiosities until he is tired. Take away the public buildings from Washington and it does not meet my expectations. The buildings are not as elegant as I expected.

General Scott remarked in his speech on the fourth of July that we would be home for Christmas Dinner. If such a happy circumstance should occur I propose to eat it with you, if it is agreeable. Oh, how pleasant will that time be when our flag has again been restored and I shall return to friends. Hoping I shall receive a letter from you in a day or two. I remain, as ever, your true friend and admirer. My address now is

> Seymour Dexter
> 23rd Regiment NY Vol.
> Care of Capt. N.B. Fowler
> Washington, DC

The following letter, although it is not dated, must have been written some time after the 16th and before the 19th, as the envelope was dated July 20th, 1861. All the delayed mail from Elmira has finally shown up. He tells of the blackberry excursions into the woods. There have been passes issued except one and that time was spent berry picking.

> Camp Diven
> 23rd Regiment New York
>   Vols.
> Washington, DC
> Camp Stationery   No Date

Dear Ellie:

Last Thursday afternoon at 6 o'clock the ladies from Elmira, through a delegation sent here for that purpose, presented to our regiment a magnificent stand of Colors. The presentation speech was made by Alexander Diven MC from Elmira. It was responded to by Col. Hoffman who made a very good reply. Old Abe, Seward and several prominent men of the nation were present. The scene was imposing and one long to be remembered. After the exercises were over our regiment was reviewed by the President and Sec. Seward. They were very highly pleased with the appearance of the regiment.

This afternoon we pass in review for Gov. Morgan. How long we shall stay after these reviews are over I do not know. There has been

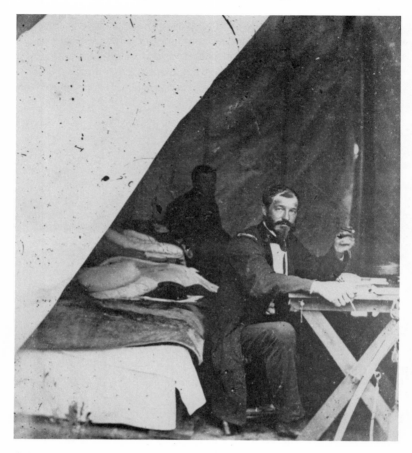

Col. Henry C. Hoffman, 23rd New York Volunteer Regiment, Elmira, N.Y. (courtesy National Archives).

some talk of our going to the Navy Yard. If we go it will be a permanent position and if the forces that are in Virginia now should be triumphant we would never see an engagement but then it is only talk. We may be ordered into Virginia within four days. I almost wish it could be so. After taking out the interludes I have already mentioned, camp life has been very monotonous for the past week. I believe I told you in my last letter that we had hired a cook;

[The rest of the letter is missing]

The review referred to in the above letter by Seymour occurred on July 17th. President Lincoln and Secretary of State Seward first reviewed the regiment, followed by the presentation of the Stand of Colors to the regiment. Col. H. C. Hoffman in his acceptance speech remarked that "it might forever float as free as the wind which unfurls it."

Journal

From our first arrival at this place rumors had been constantly afloat that we were to cross the Potomac in a few days, but they all proved false, much to our disappointment. For a long time the press and public opinion had been crying out "Onward, Onward" and the New York Tribune had placed at the head of its columns as the exponent of its sentiments "Onward to Richmond before the 20th (of July)." No doubt being influenced much by popular opinion which charged the government with being too tardy in its movements and an advance was begun about the 17th, led on by Gen. McDowell who was commander of the division across the river. The enemy was stationed in considerable force at Fairfax Courthouse but their main army was fortified at Manassas Junction. It was the intention of McDowell to advance as to give them battle on the 19th, but from obstructions found in the road and in the inexperience of the army in marching he was not able to do it. As our forces approached Fairfax Court the enemy retreated towards Centerville and as our army advanced from there to Bull Run upon the 18th a detachment under Gen. Tyler was sent forward on a reconnaissance. They had a sharp skirmish with some of the advance forces of the enemy and drove them back. Upon the 20th the main army arrived at Centerville and prepared to give them battle on the morrow. Our troops were all in excellent spirits feeling confident of a glorious victory. But alas!! how often the highest hopes of the populace are not realized but the bitterest disappointment and chagrin takes their place. About nine o'clock on Sunday the 21st the boom of cannon in the distance was borne to our ears up the southwestern wind. The turmoil increased until about 11 o'clock. A continual roar of artillery told us that something besides a mere skirmishing was taking place. The deepest suspense lay upon the hours although not any seemed to have any fears as regard to the success of our arms. While upon dress parade, word was received that our army was being

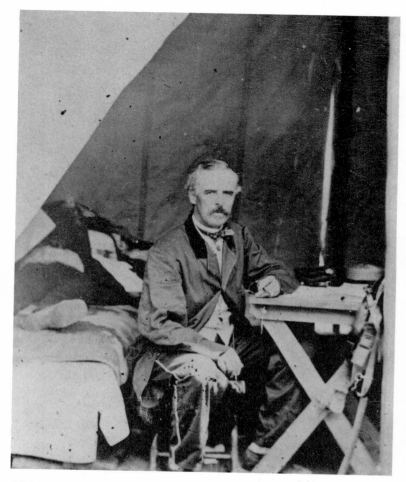

Major William M. Gregg, 23rd New York Volunteer Regiment, Elmira, N.Y. (courtesy Library of Congress).

successful and that Manassas Junction was within our grasp. The news was considered trustworthy. The regiment was drawn in to a hollow square and the tidings were communicated to us by Major Gregg who proposed three cheers. Col. Hoffman remarked that the news was too good to be true and we may have to take back our cheers. How true did his words prove. We returned to our tents with high hopes and joyous spirits. As we were preparing to retire orders came that we must have two days' rations in our haversacks and be ready to march the first thing in the morning. All was excitement and hubbub in the camp. The cooks were preparing rations for the men and some were preparing their knapsacks, others writing farewell letters home or elsewhere and still others seem to spend their time in listlessness around the camp. Little comfort was found by those wishing to sleep. At the first streak of dawning day we were called out to have our haversacks packed with the rations and finish packing the haversacks. Our muskets had been exchanged for Enfield rifles and with our new Stand of Colors that had been presented to the regiment. It wasn't long before a suspicion lurked in the hearts of very many that a reverse had taken place upon the battle field and we were being driven back for it. If not, then why all this bustle on this side of the river since we had noticed that the camps surrounding us had received similar orders. The morning wore away and we wondered why the drums did not beat for us to fall in but by and by it passed around that our orders were only to hold ourselves in readiness to march. We were some chagrined at this. The lowering heavens had threatened rain since daybreak and as we began to mount guard it commenced to rain which it kept up until midnight without cessation. It was our guard and I think it was one of the gloomiest days I have ever seen. The forenoon passed without getting any reliable news from the scene of carnage but about noon Prof. Allen came up to us. He had been a spectator of the sanguinary engagement, being with the Sherman battery in the center column. Now we learned the fact that we were totally defeated and our forces left the field in utter confusion. Our army which 48 hours before had been advancing, stimulated by patriotism, strengthened by the justness of their cause and joyful in the hope of a certain and brilliant victory were now retreating with blasted hopes, disgraced arms and gloomy spirit.

Never before had the stars and stripes been so dishonored. It struck a blow that fell deep upon the hearts of loyal Americans. Freedom arrayed itself in "sackcloth and ashes" while slavery dressed itself in the gaudiest apparel and rejoiced amid music and the roar of saluting cannon. Our men had fought bravely, marching up to the cannons mouth with a heroism, challenging our admiration, driving the enemy from post to post, taking one redoubt after another until nearly 5 p.m. when the victory seemed inclined to us. But at this critical juncture Johnson of the rebels arrived with fresh legions who proved too strong for our already exhausted troops. The reserves for some reason not being brought up to support, nothing was left for them except to retreat. It seems we have underrated the resources and arms of the south and that there was some incompetency among our officers.

Washington was now wide open for possible taking by the rebels and the troops surrounding and near Washington were ordered to close in tightly about the Capitol. At noon the next day we were ordered to strike our tents and prepare to march. In an hour the baggage and wagons were set to roll and we marched towards Washington. On all sides we could see relics and effects of the disaster. Soldiers were scattered in every direction most with soiled and torn clothes and many with an arm in a sling. They expressed wishes that we would never be obliged to retrace their steps. In crossing the long bridge we met several ambulances conveying the wounded to the city. Our regiment was halted at Camp Runyon at the end of the bridge and we pitched our tents a few rods from the fort on some even ground. It was expected that the rebels would advance following up on their victory and we would be obliged to give battle. All expectations were disappointing in this direction. We believe that the rebels at the time thought that the retreat was a feint and were afraid that a trap was being set for them. It was also possible that the enemy had been so severely whipped that they were not able to recoup enough to continue to Washington.

Arlington Heights
July 24, 1861

My Dear Friend:

From the heading of this letter you will perceive that we have moved our camp. We moved yesterday afternoon and we are now encamped upon Virginia soil. Already you have heard of the defeat at Bull Run and no doubt you are anxious to know whether your Alfred friends were in that engagement or not, that and other reasons I write this short letter to you now. As regards to the battle, I do not know what kind of coloring the northern papers may put upon it, but it was utter defeat and complete rout. Our arms were disgraced, not by courage of the men, but by the incompetency of the field officers.

You may be some surprised to hear that Prof. Allen was in this battle but that was the case. He was in the center column with

Professor Jonathan Allen, president of Alfred University, 1867–1892 (courtesy Alfred University Archives).

Sherman's Battery until 5 o'clock in the afternoon. He then started for home, at the time the field was ours, but soon after that the retreat commenced and shortly a complete rout. Of course, he was there as a spectator, but he was in just as much danger as the men working in the battery. The Union Regiment was in the hottest of the battle in which there is some Alfred students, George Utter, Clinton Lewis and Banks. They are all safe unless it is Banks. I have not heard from him yet but trust that he is not injured. The rebels showed no mercy. They bayoneted the wounded as they lay helpless upon the ground. There is one incident barbarous enough to make a civilized man blush for humanities sake. A person found a wounded friend who was helpless so he laid his gun down by his side and went for assistance. When he came back he found his own bayonet run through his friend and sticking in the ground with the gun up. This is but one of the many deeds of barbarism.

The 26th Reg., the one in which Clark is in, crossed into Virginia last Sunday, the day of the battle, hence they did not arrive in time to be in the battle, but they may now have been engaged since that for aught I know. They must be near the enemy lines and undoubtedly will be in the next battle. The enemy are advancing and I understand that they are at Fairfax Court House now, which is only 20 miles away. Hence, we are liable to be called into battle within 36 hours. Of course, it will depend upon the movements of the enemy—if they continue to advance we have got to come out immediately and we will meet them.

Ellsworth Zouaves in the battle fought with a desperation almost bordering upon frenzy. They would rush up to the enemies' entrenchments and seize a rebel and drag him over the bank and cut his throat. They almost annihilated the black cavalry, which proved so disastrous to a portion of our troops.

Our regiment are all in good spirits at the prospect of a fight. We are all in good health with exception of Chapin who is still some feeble. While I am writing to you, a large balloon up almost over us, is making observations of the enemy.

My dearest friend, how I should like to see you this morning. It is a beautiful morning and I can imagine just how it looks around home this morning. My mother is thinking of me and wondering whether her only son is still living or not. He is now, but may not be in 24 hours from this time. The future surely is covered over with dark clouds around which I cannot perceive except with the eyes of faith. You spoke in one of your letters about no one but myself reading your letters. Surely, my dear no one other than mine eyes peruse them. I shouldn't tho consider it a betrayal of a trust and confiding heart to the gaze of others who may make it a subject of ridicule. My heart is filled with emotion as I gaze to the northward and think of home and friends. Not with emotions of regret, for I do not wish to return until the disgrace which our arms have suffered has been wiped away.

It is now time for affection to rule the heart, stern duty points the way and he is no man who will not follow it.

God only knows if I fall. One of my friends will let you know as soon as possible. All I ask in that case is for you to ever remember me as a brother friend and one that died doing his duty and at length meet me in heaven.

Your Brother Friend
Seymour

Letter was franked by N.A. Harris. Postmarked Washington D.C., August 10, 1861.

Arlington Heights
August 4, 1861
Sunday Eve

My Dear Friend:

In compliance with your request I send you all your letters which I have had since Elmira. I lost two or three of them some way. Ellie, I send these letters expecting that you will preserve them at least until you hear that I have fallen. If I should ever return to meet you again I expect that you will return them to me. In them are many sentiments that have been a comfort and also giving me pleasure, believing them to come, as I do, from a heart true to its professions and noble in its aspirations.

My main reason for writing tonight and sending you the letters is that we have received our marching orders tonight. We are to make an advance. We strike our tents at 8 o'clock tomorrow morning. We are going to the front lines, 205 men from our regiment have been appointed an advance guard and I am one of the number. Continue to direct your letters as here-to-fore and I hope to receive them as frequently as before.

Your Friend,
Seymour

Letter franked by ?—name illegible.

Arlington Heights
August 8, 1861

Although my letter is dated from Arlington, as here-to-fore, still we are about three miles in advance of the place that we occupied before. Arlington Heights is a large tract of land owned by General Lee. It is said to contain 18,000 acres. Our camp is in the midst of

Camp scene, 23rd Regiment, Company E, unidentified soldiers (courtesy National Archives).

woods. The trees and brush had to be cut off before we could pitch our tents. We are about 6 miles from some of the enemy encampments. Pickets are sent out daily. A party went out yesterday on a scouting mission, they fell in with some enemy cavalry with whom they had a skirmish. Some of the enemy was killed, but none of our men injured.

Arlington Heights are almost impregnable as a fortress from below Alexandria to far above Georgetown. A large amount of land is covered by a dense forest. These are being cut down for a double purpose. First, so that they can plant batteries upon the most commanding position and, second, the fallen forest will be a great impediment to the advance of the enemy should they drive into our front lines. It has fallen to my lot to chop two days since we have been here and I confess that there is not much poetry in chopping beneath Virginia now a days.

Brother,
Seymour

Journal

This is a pleasant camping ground as far as the surrounding view is concerned but its proximity to the marshes of the Potomac and also the canal that passed along its front made it subject to miasmatic fevers and the special abode of mosquitoes, which were the most persevering enemies that we had yet met. To the north of us lay the valley of the Potomac obscure from our view for a great distance by woods, across the river spread out in plain view was the city with all its surroundings. It was a beautiful sight to behold upon a clear morning as the first rays of the rising sun came over the far distant hills and kissed the still waters of the river from which they rose reflected as from a mirror. Away to the south flowed the river upon whose bosom almost constantly might be seen the trailing smoke of the steam tug or the sails of the schooner and now and then the more majestic form of a man-of-war, from whose sides salutes from the thundering cannon pealed for the arrival or departure. On the west not far distant rose the heights of Arlington upon one of the most commanding elevations of which stood a strong and wide commanding fort known as "Fort Albany." To the north of it upon another high elevation stood the mansion of Gen. Lee who had owned the tract of land known as Arlington Heights but now had forfeited his claim by disavowing the Stars and Stripes and accepting a commission in the Southern Confederacy. Our camp is on the main road from the bridge. We see nearly all the troops that pass over the river. Continual wagon trains, baggage cars and wagons pass over the bridge with numberless regiments on the way to the front or to set up camp in the area.

Our company is very much dissatisfied with company cooking on Meridian Hill. It was decided that we would cook by squads, the inmates of a tent forming a squad. We lived much better than when we all cooked together. It gave each one a chance to economize and prepare the rations to suit himself.

A week has gone by and no enemy has been near to molest us. The night of the 28th there was an alarm. The long roll beat in all the surrounding camps and in less than ten minutes the regiment had formed the line of battle and 20 rounds of ammunition were distributed to each man. Nearly all thought that enemy was near at hand because it was the first time we had ever been called out in the night. After keeping us in line for an hour the Col. dismissed us and sent us to our tents. We found the next day that the whole thing had been gotten up on purpose to get the regiments accustomed to forming a line of battle in the night. This was the first and last that we had an alarm as such again.

Arlington Heights
August 18, 1861

Dear Sister Ellie:

It is Sunday afternoon and a disagreeable time indeed. It has been raining five days out of the last six, keeping it all around our tents nothing but mud, from which a nuisance arises which that it is very unhealthy and is telling its effects on the men.

There were 17 in our company this morning sick so as to be unfit for duty. A good share of them are sick with what we call here the Virginia Fever, but what is called in New York a Bilious Remittent Fever. It is a specie of fever and again I am afraid that it is going to be very prevalent in camp. The doctor told me today that there are 56 cases in camp at present. If the rainy weather continues the sick list will increase. Two died the day before yesterday, one from an injury caused by a falling tree upon him while engaged in chopping; the other one had measles and mumps and caught a severe cold on top of them. These have been the first deaths that have occurred since the regiment has been together.

We have been chopping trees in camp in order for the sun to shine upon us if it ever comes out again.

The next few days were spent on picket duty. The guards have been getting their fill of fresh peaches and fruit that abound in the area farms.

The 23rd, 25th, 35th and the 37th have been formed into a brigade under Col. Sedgwick to be held in reserve, and to be stationed near Arlington Heights.

Our supper will be ready in a few minutes. Brown is the chief cook and I will give him the credit of being an excellent one. How would you like to take a peek at us as we partake of a few franks and beans?

The area that we have been doing picket duty is over 6 walking miles and about 2-1/2 straight miles. It does break the monotony of camp life. After setting our post the other day we went out to explore a neighboring corn field and we returned with corn which we roasted for our dinner. The enemy is about 1-1/2 miles from our advance picket line. There is a big peach orchard between us.

It rained most of the time and still kept drizzling come nightfall, hence we had to manage some way to keep off the rain. Tommy Sanders and myself were together, so taking some rails from a fence we put an end on a fence and the other upon the ground and over these we spread a large rubber blanket which served as a roof, then we spread a blanket underneath on the wet ground, laying our cartridge boxes down for a pillow and taking another blanket apiece, we rolled up in them and laid down to rest. As soon as daylight came we had to get up and go out to reconnoiter in different areas. While Capt. Chapman went near the peach orchard with no enemy in sight, all at once there was a volley of musket and balls came a whizzing all around them. They made a fast retreat and no one was injured. The rebels were concealed in the bushes. Capt. Fowler's Co. K group received the same treatment. All we returned with and run into was lots of peaches which we brought back for the men to enjoy.

A spy came into camp today and said that the enemy was withdrawing their troops farther back, leaving a small force of cavalry on the frontier for picket duty.

It is evening now and our squad are all sitting around writing letters and it is getting quite late and tattoo is just beating for us to go to bed. They are playing "The Girl I Left Behind Me"! That's one of the tunes they always play at tattoo, it turns my thoughts a long ways from here.

Your Brother,
Seymour

The falling tree incident referred to in the letter was a quirk of fate. James Pease of Company E, while on a working party felling a tree, was struck by a falling limb that injured him so badly he died of a brain concussion.

Camp scene, 23rd Regiment, Company K (courtesy National Archives).

Arlington Heights
Sept. 8, 1861

Dear Ellie:

With a heart filled with the deepest grief do I write today. One of the noblest of our Alfred land will be no longer numbered among the living. The spirit of Lucius Bacon at a quarter past six last Friday morning quit its tenement of day and so we firmly believe winged its way to a land of eternal rest. He fell not upon the battlefield but by a withering hand of disease. His death was unexpected to all. No one of us considered him dangerous while in camp. One week ago last Friday we removed him to Columbia College hospital, two miles to the north of the city, where he would receive better treatment than could be possible to give him in camp. Last Wednesday Thatcher and Brown visited him when they entertained to fear of his death but strong hopes of an immediate recovery with the care he was receiving. We should have visited him every day but the expectation of immediate battle kept us in camp. No passes being granted to pass the river. Yesterday through a letter by way of Prof. Boyles we learned that although the doctor thought him better upon Thursday, still Bacon thought he must die. On these grounds I managed to get a pass but judge my feelings upon arriving at the hospital and finding that he had died and been buried the day before without an old friend near. His disease was the remittent fever of the typhoid type. He was buried at the soldiers home where his remains will remain unless his friends wish them sent home. He was a noble young man loved by all with whom he came in contact. He was a true Christian and a brave soldier.

I presume you have learned from the newspapers that an attack upon us has been expected during the past week. We have been prepared to march at a moments notice; it may be another week before an advance is made by one side or the other. In my last letter I told you that the press has been shut out from camp. They have again made their appearance. Our squad has sent for the Daily Tribune so that we get the news regular now.

My heart is sick,
Seymour

Arlington Heights
Sept. 15, 1861

Classmate and Friend:

I presume you have seen the order in the papers issued by Gen.
McClellan as regards to the Sabbath. The order meets with a hearty
welcome in the army and I am sure it cannot fail of finding a response
in the heart of every true patriot in the north whether he be Christian or skeptic. We have church services tonight at half past seven o'clock.

The smooth ground will be our pews and the broad canopy of
nature our church and the silver moon our light. It would be so roman-
tic were there not so much wickedness around.

Nothing much of importance has happened in the vicinity the
past week, other than a skirmish or two. Last Wednesday there was a
sharp skirmish at Lewinsville. No doubt you read of it in the papers.
There was so much cannonading that we at first thought that a general engagement was underway.

The night before last the rebels succeeded in burning several
houses which have been heretofore occupied most of the time by our
pickets. One of them was Hall's house which occupied one of the most
commanding positions in this section. They undertook to burn it by
shelling some time ago, but did not succeed. The fortifications along
our lines are pretty well completed. If a general engagement should
take place along this line, it would be 7 to 8 miles long and the cannon is counted by the hundreds that would hurl forth their devastat-
ing missiles amid the deafening roar. It would be a horrible yet sublime
sight. It seems strange that freedom, truth and justice must be bought
by such a price, yet it has ever been thus. Almost every victory of freedom over tyranny has been baptised in blood.

The engagement long expected between Rosecrans and Floyd has
taken place giving a complete victory to our arms. Our cause begins
to look much brighter than it did a short time ago after the Bull Run
affair.

The stand that the legislature of Kentucky takes is truly encour-
aging and I trust that North Carolina would take almost as strong a
union stand if a sufficient number of Federal troops are introduced
there to support the union sentiment. There is so much secrecy about
all the military movements that we know nothing about what is going
on beyond our observations.

Camp scene, 23rd Regiment, Company K (courtesy National Archives).

It is getting near meeting time and I hear the drums beating for church, so I take my leave.

Seymour

Arlington Heights
September 22, 1861

Dear Ellie:

Upon Tuesday we had a brigade review and inspection by McDowell, yesterday we had a skeleton brigade drill with McDowell commanding. He passes through the camp nearly every day. He is a man about 5 ft. 10 in. in height, very broad through the chest, quite fleshy, of a sandy complexion with a round face and a short chubby nose; I should judge about 40 years of age. He has a good voice for command. Although he is a smart man, he lacks that deep-seated energy, quickness of perception and judgment necessary for a great military leader. I have not seen McClellan yet to know him, but I expect to tomorrow. No one has an idea that there will be an immediate battle along this line. It is the policy of the government, no doubt, to attack Richmond from the rear.

Seymour

At this point, while the 23rd was encamped near Arlington, the Rebels had retired to a short distance from the Federals at Upton Hill and Munson Hill, directly in on the rear of Upton. This proximity had kept the 23rd in an all-time readiness for action. Prof. Lowe's balloon ascensions were certainly effective in keeping a constant tab on enemy movements, gun emplacements and general layout of the enemy. It was only after McClellan had taken over the Munson and Upton hills, however, that they discovered the enemy's ruse. To the chagrin and hilarity of the men and officers, the so-called cannon that had them so upset were only stove pipes mounted on wheels and the earthworks and fortifications were simple furrows of earth.

Upton Hill
October 2, 1861

Dear Ellie:

Ere this I presume you have heard of the advance of a portion of our forces in this vicinity. Last Saturday afternoon about five o'clock as we were busily engaged in stopping up the cracks in our log cabin with mud, the "Long Roll" beat, which is a signal of alarm, as at least that we shall fall into line with the greatest of speed for some action with the enemy. Soon forming lines the Col. gave us orders to return to our tents and get two day's ration and 40 rounds of cartridges as quickly as possible. This was the most acceptable news we had heard in some time, since we knew there was to be some movement on the enemy. A few minutes found us again in line all equipped for the battle field. We wheeled into column and then closed up to close column. When our Col. spoke to us he said that we were going where there might be some work to be done and he wished every man to obey orders implicitly, never to leave the ranks and always to keep perfectly cool. With these admonitions he gave the orders.... Forward March! With our band playing and colors flying and all in the gayest spirits away we started for the enemy.

Going double quick time, most of the time, two miles were soon past, which brought us to where the enemy lines were in the morning but no sign of one was now to be seen. On we went double time for the next two miles, passing a railroad which you will find on the map and ascending and taking possession of the hill which we now occupy, which is in the same chain of hills with Munson and in sight of it. It was deep twilight, as we were ascending the hill we met McClellan and staff. As we neared the summit so as to look over the top against the western horizon, there were McDowell and staff and Gen. Wadsworth. They were making a reconnaissance and consulting as regarding the disposition of the forces. There was but one regiment with us. We were drawn into battle line on the summit of the hill. It was truly animating to see the officers riding backward and forward in front of the line giving orders. It had been the intention that we should sleep in arms in line of battle but after a reconnoiter it was decided that there was no imminent danger of an attack. Being very cold and having no blankets or overcoats we were excused from that and each company found its own quarters close by. They immediately sent back for our coats which arrived about midnite. By that time ten pieces of cannon were drawn up in battle array before our front and two full brigades were in the vicinity. We dare not build camp fires where we were but Gen. Keyes' brigade lay down on the east side of the hill and built an immense camp fire presenting a magnificent sight about two o'clock in the morning. Heavy firing occurred far distant on the right making a bustle among us for a time thinking that the enemy were trying to flank us. Morning broke with no sight of the enemy. Although it was Sunday, heavy detachments were sent out from each regiment to felling trees so as to give range to our cannon and make preparations to throw up breastworks. The fortifications of the enemy were mere shows. Monday morning seemed more alive, the forests were falling in every direction and forts began to rise in commanding positions.

The same thing continues and will continue until finished forts rise upon nature's battlements crowned with rifled cannon and thundering Columbias. Yesterday we moved our tents over. It seemed hard to leave our little house with all its accommodations.

Our pickets were thrown out as far as Falls Church. A deserter from the enemy lines came into the camp of the 12th New York today. He is formerly from near Syracuse, being in Tenn. on some business he was pressed into the service. He is personally known to the members of the regiment. He reports the condition of the rebels as deplorable in some things. He bears evidence of it, at least his uniform is very ragged. He says that there are many who would fly to our lines if they thought they could pass the pickets. It but corroborates what we hear from other sources. Prof. Lowe is here with his balloon and McDowell makes ascensions quite frequently. They are able to see Manassas and go up 500 and 600 feet.

Seymour

Upton Hill
October 9, 1861

My Dear Friend:

Another week of soldier life is past and again I sit down for a chat with Ellie. It is a regular October evening, a little fire would be quite acceptable as a part of the surroundings, but there is no place for a fire in a soldier's tent. If it is too cold he must "go to bed" to keep warm, that is throw his blanket over himself. Nothing of special interest has occurred along our line the past week. Three fortifications have been nearly completed in sight of our camp.

Our regiment has been at work upon one today. Several picket guards of the enemy are very easily seen from our camp by means of glasses. They have been within cannon range of us until yesterday ever since we came here. Last Saturday Sherman's battery (I believe) situated on a hill to the northeast of us, fired several shots at a party of rebels but they found that their shells fell short. The enemy made no answer until just before when they threw shells at a regiment near us. Whereupon a battery belonging to our brigade posted by the side of our camp brought a rifled cannon to bear upon them. They soon ended a willingness to quit the play by ceasing fire. It was truly animating to hear the shell as they mounted into the air, at least 200 feet at their highest elevation, and sped away nearly three miles. McClellan compliments our division on the amount of labor they have performed since we took possession of the hill. We place much confidence in McDowell and I see by the papers tonight that he is to be appointed Major General of the Vol. I hope that we shall not lose him as our division general.

Thursday night

I am glad I am not on guard duty tonight as the weather is very chilly and a fine rain is falling. The past several weeks things have been very quiet. I am now reading Dickens' "Great Expectations," to pass the time. I have become very interested in it.

> Your Brother Friend,
> Seymour

> Upton Hill
> October 20, 1861

My Friend Ellie:

It is Sunday again and I have just come off of guard duty and eaten dinner of bean soup and coffee. The routine is very monotonous and has been unchanged in the camp since I have last written. The monotony has been broken almost everyday by some startling rumors or by an exchange of shells between our lines and those of the enemy. Nearly all the men have been on guard duty every day during the past week and have worked upon a fort a short distance from our camp.

Last Thursday our camp was kept in suspense all day by startling rumors. Gen. Wadsworth and staff, with a company of cavalry and one of infantry, went out on a reconnaissance. A report was soon afloat that all had been captured. This was soon contradicted by another report that General had sent back for his brigade to advance. This proved to be true but the affair was telegraphed to McClellan and he put a stop to it and told him to return with his troops. The General went to within a half mile of Fairfax Court House, some seven miles beyond our lines. Rumors like this kept us in a state of anxiety all the time.

Brown has been on the sick list for over a week. He has typhoid fever but he is coming along alright. Lewis H. Kenyon has not been too well since his bout with the fever but he is slowly coming around (ALFRED BOYS!). Charles Chapin also has been threatened with a touch of fever but he is holding his own.

Winter is beginning to set in around us and with it its mantle of white but how different will be its association, to me at least, from what they were a year ago. How deep treasure up in my heart are the memory of those times. With much pleasure they will pass in review at times as I place my long beat at dead of night.

The two Kenyon brothers are joining the company. You ask if I think I could re-enter upon my studies again at the end of two years with the same interest as when I left them. I certainly think I can. The "trip," if I survive it will surely give me a realizing sense of the great advantages that a student there enjoys.

It is time to go on guard duty again so I must bring this to a close. My heart could speak much more but another duty calls. As ever remember me as

Your true friend & brother
Seymour

Cold weather was starting to set in and the men were forbidden to set fires; nights were cold and bleak and the days, chilling the soldiers' bones to the marrow, left an indelible mark on those who, as yet, had not reached the stage where they could endure in the hills, especially without ample clothes and blankets. Sickness among the men was beginning to increase at an alarming rate. It was at this camp that the men started to clean out the brush and trees and set up fortifications and defense

lines for the protection of the Capitol. After cutting down numer-
ous trees, they proceeded to make little cabins for living in. Tents
did not suffice for protection against the cold wind and blow-
ing snows. So, it was apropos that a presentable camp was built
of little log cabins set neatly side by side, with and without
small fireplaces attached. It was in cabins, such as they were,
that the soldiers were able to acclimate themselves better to the
bitter sting of winter. The months of December, January and
February slowly moved on and the soldiers found themselves in
a constant round robin of drills, reviews and infernal picket
duty. Notwithstanding the fact that they found themselves ever-
lastingly called out for a quick march somewhere because of rumors
that were always with them, the general health of the regiment
did immensely improve during these months of arduous rigid
training, occasional good food and relatively comfortable quar-
ters. It all added to making the 23rd a well-disciplined regiment.

Ellie is now through at Alfred and is teaching school in
Burlington Flats in Otsego County, N.Y. Seymour is undecided
as to what he is going to do if he ever is lucky enough to sur-
vive this terrible crisis that he is now engaged in. His parents
want him to continue on at Alfred but, like all young men, he
is not sure at this point what he wants to do and still keep his
parents in good stead.

Upton Hill
October 26, 1861

My Dear Friend:

Another week of labor with us, not upon fortification but in
drilling. During the forenoon we had battalion or company drills and
a part of the time a march with knapsacks on in the afternoon. We
have been under marching orders all the week. That is to hold ourselves in readiness to march at a moments notice with three days'
rations. Our last defeat at Balls Bluff was sad indeed. Affairs like that
strike upon the soldier's heart. They shake his confidence in the leaders by whose blunders his own life may be thus sacrificed. America
might well drape herself in mourning when the noble Baker fell while
at the head of his brigade upon the battlefield. None were more brave

Camp scene, 23rd Regiment, Company E (courtesy National Archives).

upon the senate floor, none more eloquent than he in maintaining the right and the integrity of his country.

I am alone in my tent tonight. Thatcher is taking care of Brown who is much improved but still wants someone by him all the time. Charles Chapin still has the run of the fever. My health has been fair the past few weeks but I haven't missed any duty.

Kenyon is better. I have a severe headache tonight as I write. You seem to think that Brown looks cross in the photograph. I think it true to nature. H.R. Maxson and Barney were at Alfred this term. I should advise Howell and every other young man of his qualifications not to enter the army as a private, at least in artillery companies.

I would advise him thus because he can labor for his country in a broader field. He might have the talent of a Webster and upon the battlefield, if he were a private he would be no more than the lowest soldier that could shoot a gun as well as he. No pure mind can like to be a soldier, but love for his country and duty may serve him to meet every hardship without a murmur that he may again see the integrity of his country restored and the right maintained.

Sunday Eve

I am alone again. It has been a beautiful day. Gentle autumnal wind has swept over hill and dale, fanning the leaves from the chestnut and oaks. But how unlike Sunday it has been in our camp. I went to church at the usual time and only about fifteen came and not an officer among the numbers. Oh, how I would like to spend one Sunday in civilized life. My dear sister Ellie, I had intended to converse with you much tonight but my heart aches so that it is impossible. I almost begin to fear that a fever is trying to settle upon me. I will answer the last part of your letter as soon as I can.

Pardon this very poor letter of not laying it to the heart but inability.

Your brother
Seymour

Upton Hill
November 5, 1861

Dear Ellie:

Nothing of importance has happened since my last letter, except last Saturday we had one of the most terrific storms I have ever experienced. It came from the east and many an unlucky soldier suddenly found themselves roofless in the beating storm. The winds hurled the tents from the pinnings as though they were toys. It raised the Potomac so that teams have not yet been able to cross either by brigade or ferry. There was to have been a grand review by McDowell today but the storm put a delay indefinitely. We do not think as it looks now that we will see any fighting this fall in these parts.

Brother,
Seymour

Upton Hill
November 27, 1861

My Dear Friend:

It is Wednesday evening as I seat myself to write to you. It has been a wet and gloomy day but tonight seated as we are in our tent by an easy fire, all seems cheerful. The past nine days have been busy days with the regiment. We have been playing soldier in good earnest. One week ago last Monday our brigade, with two others of McDowell's divisions, were reviewed by him on the review grounds which lie between Munson Hill and Bailey's Cross Roads about a mile and a half from our camp. On the next day the same number of troops were on the grounds nearly all day, clearing it of constructions and preparing it for the grand review which took place the next day, an account of which I presume you have already read in the papers. One week ago this morning with knapsacks on and haversacks containing our dinner, we formed a line at 8 o'clock and we were marching to the grounds. Our brigade was among the first there but already every road leading to the place was pouring in a dense mass of troops, artillery and cavalry. The position in which it happened to be our lot to be placed was unfavorable to getting a fine view of the vast concourse as they were stationed in line in their respective divisions before the grand review began. At twelve o'clock General McClellan and staff, the President and Sec. Seward and a large number of prominent men both of civil and military order rode upon the field. Nearly all the cannon present poured forth their thundering salutes, fairly making the ground tremble beneath our feet, as they rode among the lines cheer after cheer arose for the General. At length, with his suite, he took his position and the troops began to pass in review. Before he left that place 90 regiments of infantry, 20 batteries of artillery numbering over a hundred pieces and 9 regiments of cavalry had passed before his scrutinizing gaze. It was one of the most magnificent sights I ever beheld. Although our knapsacks began to take some of the poetry off before night. There is a grandeur that makes one feel inspired as he beholds such a mighty concourse armed and equipped and ready to take to the field of battle to defend their country's rights. Last Friday our regiment went out on picket duty. It happened to be the lot of our company to be placed upon the most advanced posts. Picket duty is very disagreeable now indeed, say nothing of the danger which attends it.

Being placed by the side of woods, in places best suited to get a view in the front, we have nothing to protect us from the inclemency of the weather. We have been out the past two days. The first night it rained and in the morning the wind came in from the north and the first snow of the season fell. The second day it was very cold and it snowed a little. We were relieved by another company and fell back as one of the reserves. It's no delightful task in the night in some concealed spot, yet where you could have a good view with rifle in hand, watching for "secesh" (secessionists).

On Tuesday, before we went out, the rebels had attacked the 12th regiment there performing picket duty and killed two or three and took some prisoners. I saw where they fell. Then when we were relieved of picket duty Monday morning by the NY 21st, we received orders together with the reserve force of the 21st NY, to protect a foraging party. We went out 1-1/2 miles beyond our lines; we picked up 17 wagon loads of forage, 25 head of cattle and we came back to camp very tired after four days of picket duty. On returning to camp that night we received orders to be ready to march at 8 in the morning and take nothing but our dinner. At 8 in the morning we formed line and started towards Fairfax, in company with two other regiments we went halfway and placed ourselves in ambush sending a small force of cavalry to entice out the rebel cavalry which so much infests our pickets. But, it failed its purpose and staying there until nearly night we returned, not having even seen a rebel today.

It has been a long time since I wrote to you before the past week but I haven't been able to do so. There has been nothing of interest and, as usual, the camp life is very dull and other than picket duty, very boring. Tomorrow is Thanksgiving and again I will spend it away from home. I should not dislike to sit down to a table richly laden with roast turkey and the like. Maybe next year.

Your Brother,
Seymour

Many entries in the journal for the months of August and September were rambling thoughts and feelings concerning factual activities of the regiment and the course of action being taken by the Union armies.

There was some rather deep concern considering the

blockades of the waterways leading into the Virginias. Seymour mentions the fact that the enemy had begun to become trouble-some along the lower Potomac: "They had several batteries near Acquia Creek landing and were fast placing them upon com-manding points up and down the river. In a short time these could become so formidable as to efficiently blockade our own craft. When the blockade of the Potomac was first hinted at as being one of the points for which the enemy was striving it was to be counted as being something they could never attain or something our government would never allow. But, as the enemy advanced in the work of blockading, the idea became less terrible and at length it was finally accomplished and we sit down to it as unconcerned as though nothing had happened. There may be some strategical reason why this has been allowed but it seems very strange that our government should allow the one water communication between its Capitol and the seaboard to be thus obstructed without making an attempt to stop it."

Journal

The regiment is elated over the news that General Buften's Division defeated the enemy at Cape Hatteras. The Federals took two forts and recaptured an equal number of cannon that they had lost at Bull Run. The news of a victory always inspired new vigor and joy among the boys in the camp.

The news of the attack on Port Royal by Commodore Dupont again gave added encouragement to the union forces. On November 7th, 1861, Forts Walker and Beauregard were reduced to submission and added to the base of operations for the Union armies.

From the seaboard let us turn our attention to the west where most of the activity was being placed in the field. J.C. Fremont's appointment as commanding general of the Mississippi Valley was hailed as a wise and judicious choice. When he took command in person the deepest interest and highest expectations were aroused in regards to his movements. In a short time and out of the disorder which was complete in the western department he organized and equipped a good army and prepared them to take to the field. In the battle of Springfield which occurred soon after his arrival he lost his most experienced and, no doubt, ablest general in the death of Gen. Lyon.

Although our forces drive the enemy from the field yet it was such a sacrifice that it could not hardly be called a victory. Again, in the surrender of Lexington he lost a brave Colonel.

Under the disadvantageous circumstances which limited his movements he was not able to fulfill the high expectations that had been raised. Disappointed politicians and those who had not received the bounties of Uncle Sam as freely as they had desired and consequently were envious of Fremont in his present position began to castigate him and charge him with inefficiency to fill the high place he held so honorably. But Fremont was a man that carried the heart of the soldier with him. He inspired confidence in the bosom of those whom he led and the energy and determination which had always characterized his actions had inspired a confidence in the people and when it was first intimated that Fremont was not the man for the position it was cast back as a base libel. When the charges were at last preferred against him by the government it led to an investigation and finally his removal. The heart of the people are still with him and believe that it was envy and jealousy that has undermined and hurled him down from the position.

Whether he is really innocent or guilty is yet to be decided in a court of inquiry. He was succeeded by Gen. Hunter who very shortly afterwards was restricted in his command, a greater portion of it being given to Gen. Halleck, one of the four Major Generals of the Regular Army.

Getting back to our own position in Upton, November 1st finds us with fortifications complete and ready to advance. The weather had been very good so no complaints on that score. Again it has been drills, marches and more picket duty to add to the joys of camp life. With each succeeding storm we were beset with an increase of flying leaves and the decaying beauties of nature upon all sides betokened the close proximity of winter. "Necessity" the mother of invention began to set the yankee genius at work to construct some means of securing the tents. It was accomplished in various ways but the most common was to dig down in the ground. From there they would dig out and around the tent and add a flue, line it with stone and build a chimney out of sod or by placing two barrels one upon another. This crude construction served to warm the tents and keep the ground dry and warm.

Sunday, the 9th, the Chaplain held services at Falls Church. Nearly all the men went, more, I guess, out of curiosity and novelty than from a desire to attend church. We carried our arms which were stacked in front of the building. This church which gives the name to the hamlet around it and has obtained such a notoriety in the present struggle, is a brick building of medium size and nearly square. It is very plain in its outside appearance and also within. There is nothing very peculiar to attract your attention. It is its age and association connected with it that gives it its sacredness which, in fact, has almost entirely shielded it from devastation. It was built in 1708 by the Episcopal denomination. The bricks were imported from England. Hence, it is one of the oldest buildings in the country. It was the resort of George Washington frequently to worship upon the Sabbath Day.

Rodney Steele, a second lieutenant of the Co., had been given furlough to return to Elmira. While in Elmira he contacted remittent fever and died Dec. 7, 1861. Lt. Steele was the first officer casualty of Co. K. He was well liked among his officers and the men held him in very high regard.

Again a deep lull has set in the camp. Winter quarters are not all it is cracked up to be and for some reason it is still drills, inspections, picket duty and an occasional march to keep the boys in shape with inclement weather.

Seymour closes his Journal 1861 with the following remarks in referring to the Steamship Trent affair with Commander Wilkes of the San Jacinto and Mason & Slidell.

Through the wisdom of the administration and the statesmanship of the Secretary of State it was amicably settled by the surrender of the fellows (Mason & Slidell). In the surrender they established a point in international law for which we had long contended.

THUS ended the campaign of 1861. Instead of having seen Richmond we have not hardly got out of the original lines of the District of Columbia, but one year from this date we trust that we can write the obituary of treason.

End of Journal

Winter Quarters
Near Munson Hill

Near Munson Hill, Va.
Dec. 15, 1861

My Dear Friend:

I am seated in my little Palace to write to you. Perhaps you will not understand the word palace, so I shall explain ... since my last letter we have moved to so-called winter quarters. We are a distance of about 3/4 of a mile from and in the rear of Munson Hill in a very pleasant place sequestered from the breath of winter winds by the surrounding hills and woodlands. Our palaces are built of logs to the height of 4 to 5 feet, with a tent put on for a roof. Many have stoves to warm them while others have fireplaces. Our squad have built the latter which is burning brightly and gives a cheerful appearance to our home as I write. If you could see us now you would think us a happy family. Lewis Kenyon is seated opposite me reading Beecher's sermons. William P. Maxson is at my side writing a letter to Skip Norton in Elmira. If you could look into our bookcase you could see, aside from papers, Great Expectations, The Pickwick Papers, David Copperfield, Rob Roy, Ivanhoe and a few other books that we have managed to pick up.

Yesterday afternoon we had a sham battle with blanks under the command of Gen. McDowell with three brigades and three batteries on the field. From the rumors it seems we will have something other than a sham fight.

Last week I spent two days in the city and I saw some of the Alfred boys who are in the 85th. NY Vol. It seemed good to see someone from home. Mail is slow and anymore runs into delays but keep writing. Tonight I must go back on guard duty and it is very cold but comfortable.

Good night
Seymour

William P. Maxson was the author of the book Campfires of the 23rd, *published in 1863. This book, written under the name of Pound Sterling, depicts the complete history, life and struggles of the 23rd. NY Vol. Regt. from May 1861 until May 1863.*

The 85th New York Volunteer was mustered in at Elmira December 1861 for a period of three years. In 1864 the 85th was ordered to Plymouth, N.C., on an assumingly minor expedition. They were obliged to surrender to superior forces and almost the entire regiment was taken prisoner. A loss of life in prison camp was appalling—222 deaths during imprisonment were reported. The 85th was also earlier actively engaged in the battles of Williamsburg and Fair Oaks, suffering a loss of 79 men killed in action, wounded and missing.

Near Munson Hill, Va.
December 25, 1861

My Dear Friend:

Darkness has descended upon the earth. Aeolus (master of the Winds * Greek Mythology) has his winds snugly chained in their caves tonight. Hardly a cloud floates to dim the azure deep from out which peeps myriads of stars. From a distance comes the sound of music. It is a brass band playing the popular army pieces. The band is now playing "tattoo," a signal to retire, but I have not yet learned to heed such rules. All seems happy around. from the amount of song and laughter I hear. Why should they not?? it's Christmas. Within our cabin all is quiet and the fire burns pleasantly in the fireplace. We are all letting our minds wander over the past and contemplating on the future. There has been no duty for a couple of days and I have spent my time reading Ivanhoe and I'm sure that the time has been well spent. The weather has been very cold and the romance of picket duty is "played out." We come back very tired.

Rumor has it that we are getting ready for another movement but profiting from past experience, we place little reliance on what we hear.

Merry Xmas
Seymour

Camp McDowell, Va.
January 19, 1862

Dear Ellie,

Pat, pat, pat, strikes the rain upon the canvas roof as I sit myself to write. If I step out of doors there is a danger of becoming stuck in the "sacred soil" and it is so adhesive in its qualities that when I come in again such a quantity is transferred that I fear it will take but a few such experiments to fill our little cabin. Camp life is now becoming a more stereotyped routine that has been hardly broken. Last Monday was payday and is characteristic of the 23rd. It's always a pleasant episode especially to those who have spent their last buck. The old saying "Money is the root of all evil" seems to manifest here. Before payday there is little drinking but since, it is visible by the bloated faces and bloodshot eyes, foolish stares, demeaning and brutish acts of degradation. To counteract this, a division of the Sons of Temperance has been organized with about 50 members among whom some have formerly been the most abject subject of this foul fiend and serpentine charmer. I sincerely trust it may prove a blessing to the regiment but I have little faith in the pledge of him who has so lost the dignity of man as to wallow in the slough of intemperance.

Last Thursday I was again on picket duty. According to custom, at half past eight found us with our blankets, knapsacks and one day's rations in our haversack consisting of fat pork and bread which is furnished in abundance by Uncle Sam. Then, a four mile walk over muddy roads brings us out into the edge of the forests. There has been heavy cannonading down the river which seems to come from the gunboats on the river.

Brown was over tonight to bid us farewell. He is going on recruiting duty and has been promoted to 2nd Sergeant. It means six more months of duty.

Camp scene, 23rd Regiment, Company K. From left: 1st Sgt. Duane Thompson, 4th Sgt. Judd Burt, 4th Corp. Lorenzo Howe, 1st Corp. Joseph Roe (courtesy National Archives).

The press is advocating that this rebellion will be crushed in two more months but I don't believe it. Yet, I do think that by July, I am confident, that the contest will have been decided.

Seymour

The Siege of Fredericksburg

The following letters cover the events that lead to, and take in, the siege of Fredericksburg. The mail from mid–February to March 1 and mid–April is either nonexistent, lost or had been stolen.

Siege of Fredericksburg, 1862
Note: Fredericksburg

March 10. The 23rd NY Vol. left Upton Hill by way of the Leesburg Turnpike, camping out the first night three miles east of Fairfax Court House. Saturday morning they took up their march toward Manassas and arrived at Bristow the next day. I mention this because at this point the 23rd was pelted with a blinding sleet, snow and rain storm for three days. The gloom, misery and desolation certainly left a profound effect among the Federal soldiers who were ill-equipped to combat the elements, to say nothing of personal comfort and the enemy. Sleep did not come easy when the marrow was chilled and food cold. The camp guard was set up in a two mile circuit and camp fires glowed cheerfully to give warmth.

On the 16th, the regiment again took off towards Catlett Station, marching 22 miles through another pelting rain storm. They arrived at Falmouth, Va., on the 18th of April, 1862.

The rebels were at the point of moving out from Fredericksburg, destroying 23 steamers, 8 merchant vessels, a large amount of stores and cotton in the warehouses at Fredericksburg.

Camp scene, 23rd Regiment, Company K (courtesy National Archives).

Seated on a side Hill
opposite Fredericksburg
Stafford Co., Va.
April, 22, 1862

Friend Ellie:

Last week, Wednesday, the "Long Roll" beat in our camp (from which I dated my last letter) a signal to prepare in haste for a march. In less than an hour each brigade was in line all equipped. The bugle sounded the order "Forward March" and away we started, the first regiment towards Catlett Station, about seven miles distant. We soon came to a stream which we had to ford, it seems to be common, as in Va. they have no bridges. We entered rich agricultural land, one in which the ravaging hand of war had not marred its natural beauties nor robbed it of its industrial adornments. Plantation homes were scattered here and there around which there was an air of comfort though not of elegance. We arrived at the Station about 4 p.m. We encamped about 1-1/2 miles distant in a grove upon a plantation that would almost defy competition. It contains 1700 acres and was owned by a Union man who was incarcerated for a time in Richmond. We remained here until Friday morning. Thursday we marched to a hamlet called Weaversville. Nothing exciting happened except we passed many groups of slaves standing along the roadside or engaged in picking up the blankets and overcoats which the boys threw away to lighten their knapsacks. We marched about 23 miles before we camped. The day being very warm until about sundown when a heavy rain overtook us and continued until we stopped. We kept plodding along until 8 p.m. when we stopped for the night. I never was so exhausted, being completely tired out by the march besides being very hungry and wet to the skin. Stopping by the sight of wood, we soon had fires built out of the rails over which we boiled our coffee and around which we sat and ate supper. We slept until reveille after drying ourselves out and wrapping up in blankets. We are now in enemy territory. Several stragglers from General Auger's brigade, which was just ahead of us, had been taken prisoners by guerrilla bands of rebels. Fearing that our baggage train might be attacked, our regiment was put behind it as rear guard. But, no enemy showed themselves. General Auger's brigade was, as I said, just ahead of us. He had quite a skirmish with the rebel's pickets as he came in on the other side of the river. They retreated after they attempted to burn the bridge, artillery fire having been brought to bear on them to pull back, before they had a chance to burn the bridge. Having taken possession of the heights which side overlooked the place he planted his cannon and sent over a few shells and then sent up a flag of truce ordering the authorities of the city to surrender before 4 p.m. Sunday or he would shell the town. The Mayor came over and said he would hoist the stars and stripes as soon as they could be made. But our flag is not yet flying these and why the delays I cannot tell. It is now rumored that the rebels intend to dispute our crossing but I see no sign of the rebels on the opposite side.

Now and then we hear the whistle of cars in the distance and our general seems to think that the rebels are receiving reinforcements. Last night some were fearful that we would be attacked and precautions were taken against surprises but I think the true solution of the matter is we have not the forces here sufficient to run the risk of cross-ing and our ammunition is scarce, also. Our camp could be easily shelled by the enemy, if they wished, but in return our artillery would soon make the city a heap of ruins. One thing is probable, we shall not lay here many days before something will take place. Either the rebels will not stand or we shall fight them. Negroes are flocking into camp in large numbers, many who have been hired as servants to the officers. They are not much more intelligent than I expected to find them. I have not yet heard one express his opinion but what he wished to be free. The health of the men is generally good and all seem anxious for the fray to begin, which seems pending. We received no mail since we left Catlett Station. There is a rumor going around, through a rebel source, that Yorktown has been taken by our forces but as to its truth we are ignorant. (Yorktown was evacuated by the rebel forces May 3, 1962 after McClellan had spent a whole month setting up batteries and digging trenches.)

Friend
Seymour

Fredericksburg, Va.
May 13, 1862

Dear Friend:

We are still here just outside the city limits. We have not advanced towards Richmond but preparations have been steadily and rapidly progressing for such a movement. The railroad from Acquia to this place is nearly in running order. The two bridges have been thrown across the river, one by laying the timbers and planks upon canal boats and the other by using a regular pontoon bridge. Also, the railroad bridge across the river is rapidly being rebuilt. On the 6th our regi-ment received notice that it had been chosen to take possession and do patrol duty and guard the avenues of approach to the city. Eight o'clock the following morning found us in line with clothes brushed, boots blackened and brass polished. Marching across we quietly took possession and moved a standard upon the summit of one of their

Camp scene, 23rd Regiment, Company F, unidentified soldiers (courtesy National Archives).

highest buildings from which the stars and stripes were flying in the breeze, never again to be lowered by an enemy hand. The regiment was divided, each company being assigned a different locality. Guards were posted upon the corners of the principal streets and the severest discipline enforced for the maintenance of order and the protection of the citizens in their legitimate pursuits.

Although the city was thus left untrammeled by military rules, yet it seemed solitary as a charnel house. Stately blocks, but shortly since unlivened by the din of traffic, now stood with closed blinds and bolted doors. Silent as an Egyptian Catacomb. Private dwellings around which there was an air of elegance and wealth, seemed deserted. Main Street, once the seat of business, could boast of but few promenaders while nearly all save the now joyous slave who showed themselves at the windows, in the door and upon the walks, seemed as though the Lord had repeated the Egyptian Passover among them.

But, the inactivity among the citizens and especially the women is evident and the hatred for the "Yankee" seems to be acute and bitter and which the aristocratic element of the ladies fail not to show at convenient opportunities.

The Christian Banner, a paper suppressed a year ago by the secession authorities, Union in its sentiments, has resumed its publication.

Alarms have been frequent the past few days. On Saturday evening the remainder of our brigade crossed the river. Sunday afternoon a party of our cavalry while scouting captured 13 prisoners. The enemy, chafed by the boldness and success of so small a party, came forward and their cavalry drew our pickets in.

The Long Roll was sounded and several regiments thrown forward in short order. The line of battle was formed and our company and one more from the next regiment in front as skirmishers, but when the reception was all prepared for them they saw fit to decline the invitation and modestly retired, having done us no damage save the killing of one cavalry horse. All has been quiet since. During Sunday evening official intelligence was received announcing the fall of Norfolk, Portsmouth and the disabling of the Merrimac. Never did these hills around echo more hearty cheers than arose from our troops at its announcement, though it was much to the disgust of the inhabitants. Whether the enemy will make a stand in front of us is more than we can divine but, it seems to me most probable that they will fall back and not allow their retreat to be cut off by McClellan.

The shades of the enemy have closed around us and the moon is out full tonight and until again,

Your true friend,
Seymour

General Patrick had been appointed military governor of Fredericksburg, and the 23rd Infantry had been assigned the task of patrolling and guarding the city. Col. H.C. Hoffman

Camp scene, 23rd Regiment, Company A, unidentified soldiers (courtesy National Archives).

chose to use a brick building near the railroad depot for his head-quarters and he posted pickets in various strategic parts of the city.

The Fredericksburg Christian Banner *published the following in regards to the stationing of the 23rd in their city:*

Pursuant to orders of Brigadier General Patrick, on Wednesday the 7th. of May, 1862, the Southern Tier Rifles, Twenty-Third New York State Volunteers, Col. H.C. Hoffman commanding, took up its line of march from camp near Falmouth for the occupation of Fredericksburg, arriving in the city at nine o'clock a.m. Such respectful regard was paid to the sensitiveness of the inhabitants of our town as to dispense with martial music usual upon such occasions, the regiment marching to its quarters with fine and soldierly bearing. Companies were immediately detailed and dispatched to outposts guarding various approaches to the city.

The officers of this regiment—field, staff and line— are gentlemen of the highest respectability and of dignified and courteous demeanor and such has been the respectful deportment of this entire command as to elicit the most unbounded admiration and confidence of all the inhabitants of our town.

By order of Colonel Hoffman, Sergeant-Major Devoe and Color Corporal Crocker flung the time honored flag—the good old "stars and stripes"— to the breeze, at headquarters, opposite the railroad depot, immediately upon their occupation. This regiment, we learn, has been chosen for the occupation of the town on account of its high character for respect, ability and rigid discipline, and from what we have seen, we are confident a more judicious selection could not be made. Witnessing, as we do, the preservation of all personal rights and privileges, the protection of private property and the unrestricted conduct and continuance of the accustomed business pursuits of our citizens, we cannot but conclude that this war is waged by the general Government upon principles infinitely transcending in mercy all others which the world has ever known, and of which history affords no precedent or parallel.

Fredericksburg, Va. Vicinity
Fri. July 4, 1862

Dear Ellie:

It is now nine o'clock, everybody is jubilant, sky rockets are mounting with their streams of brilliant fire. Fire crackers are cracking all over the place, while now and then are explosions from heavy guns. The drums and bugles are now playing tattoo. It has been a pleasant fourth of July. At ten o'clock this forenoon our brigade was formed around a stand erected in a long beautiful field. We were to have been addressed by General King but, for some reason, he did not show up. The national salute was fired from a large howitzer. Prayers were offered and a dedication read.

July 6th—The spirit of joviality became too much for my powers

Camp scene, 23rd Regiment, Company A, unidentified soldiers (courtesy National Archives).

of concentration of the other evening as I have just finished reading of the battle before Richmond. My mind is almost bewildered by the horrors confronted, the suffering and the noble patriotic and indomitable heroism of our soldiers. That deep and terrible suspense that has held us almost spellbound for over a week has broken. The never defeated standard of McClellan rose triumphantly but the wreaths of victory are draped in mourning for the noble Sons of America whose crimson gore have dyed the earth so freely. We still have a great faith in McClellan. He is the idol of the entire army. Last winter he was assailed by the press and public opinion. It was the steadfastness for purpose and impenetrable front which he showed to these base columinaries. Had he been anything else than a noble patriot and strong minded man, a man that comprehended his task and felt himself its equal, a man that knew he was in the right and that time would reveal it, he would have attempted to hurl back those base slanders by open declaration or by immediate action. He never lost the confidence of the soldiers. His ever presence inspires one with confidence and there is no man that I want to see ride higher on the tower of fame than General McClellan.

We are camped at present about two miles from the city in a large and beautiful field and the center of our brigade is in a small grove where stands and seats have been erected for church exercises.

We are most pleased that Pope has been placed at the head of our corps and now we trust there will be something besides marching and counter marching. I have lost my faith in Fremont. I believe that ambition is the greatest pastime with him rather than patriotism. General Shields' division has left and we are the only real division left in McDowell's corps here. I presume we will not go until we go under the command of General Pope.

> Your Soldier Friend
> Seymour

> Fredericksburg, Va.
> August 9, 1862

Dear Friend:

Not knowing when another as good an opportunity may present itself for me to write, I embrace this.

We have had busy times since I wrote last. On the 24th (July) our regiment, in company with other forces, went out to reconnoiter in the area of Orange County Court House. We were gone three days and in that time we marched 80 miles. There were some skirmishes but no

Camp scene, 23rd Regiment, Company D, unidentified soldiers (courtesy National Archives).

serious fighting. It was by far the severest tramp we have endured. On the next day after our return we moved camp. General Patrick has been temporarily appointed military governor of the city. He moved a portion of his brigade across the river and the remainder he camped on the river bank opposite the city. Our company has been detailed to do guard duty in the town around the depot, foundry and other places where there are government stores. General Patrick placed the city under Martial Law. I think they are attempting to conquer the rebels by "Moral Persuasion."

There are about 10,000 troops here and Jackson has over 30,000 but the insecurity has been suddenly removed. Last Monday General Burnside's troops are beginning to move in. His coming has been kept so still that not even a rumor had preceded him. He is here now with about 20,000 (troops) of his tried veterans. General Stevens of his command has relieved General Patrick of his duties as Governor and we have joined our regt. The whole of King division is preparing to go and join Pope. Our division now has orders to begin march at 6 o'clock this afternoon. We shall directly go to either Culpeper or Orange Court House, a distance of 40 miles. The weather is unmercifully hot. The inhabitants tell us that it excels anything they have experienced for a number of years. It is intended that we march 10 miles per day. So, I think we can get along. All who are not able to march are going to be shipped to Warrenton on the cars. The health of the troops is good considering the exposures they have undergone.

General Pope has infused a new spirit into this department. His orders have sounded like war and has made his entire command feel that they are not sacrificing their lines in playing with the enemy. We all believe that something has to be done besides the march up to the vicinity of the enemy and sit down there until he gets tired and leaves. The president's new call for troops has also given new courage to the troops. No one expected to remain two years in the service when they enlisted. All expectations would be that the war would last one year at the longest, but now it is going into two years and the enemy has a larger force in the field than we shall have until the new troops arrive. Bring 600,000 troops into the field and rebellion will soon be brought to a close. My only wish is that the war be brought to a close in a few months by a complete defeat of the south. Undoubtedly our division will soon see fighting in the vicinity of Gordonsville. There is no one they would be better pleased to meet than Jackson. I expect my next letter will be in the vicinity of Gordonsville.

Seymour

Seymour's reference to the march to Gordonsville being severe is an understatement. The troops marched on a rough plank road and after marching 15 miles and having set up a bivouac for the night were pelted with one of those heavy thunderstorms that were so prevalent in Virginia. The men were thoroughly soaked. The 80 mile march was covered in three days through a wilderness, rough and rugged roads, more than usual terrible storms, the heat of the August sun and within close proximity to the enemy.

The reconnaissance was made through apparent wilderness with an occasional comfortable home or farm along the route. Now and then a family of Virginians, very poor, were found in some tumbled-down log hovel fighting off starvation.

The 23rd on the third day bivouacked about three miles from Orange Court House. Food was very scarce, the men were very weary and a large force of rebel troops were camped out near the courthouse. It was at this time that a large herd of sheep was discovered and soon became part of the evening's repast.

The next day they had hoped to take on the Rebels but, again, common sense prevailed. They were unmercifully outnumbered and, besides, it was not the object of the expedition to engage but to take reference to numbers and location. At this time the 23rd fell back for a return march and, tired as they were, they were harassed by the enemy and more thundershowers which lasted into the night.

The Second Bull Run

Upton Hill, Va.
Sept. 4, 1862

(Ref: Battle of Second Bull Run) Aug. 30, 1862
My Dear Friend:

God has spared my life unmaimed through the fiery ordeal of the last two weeks. I should have written to you but I presume you know that there was an embargo on mail, hence, it was impossible. I cannot narrate to you all the events that have transpired with us since the last letter. Time forbids and in mixing instances my pen would be but a portrayer of the reality. We did not arrive at Cedar Mountain until Monday after the battle, they had just finished burying the dead and removing the wounded. We expected an engagement the next morning after our arrival, but during the night Jackson fell back across the Rapidan. On Saturday following, we made an advance and we camped at the foot of the mountain on a portion of the battle field. During the next day I went over the whole field but I will not describe it. There are other scenes more vivid upon my mind. On the following Tuesday morning we began to fall back towards Rappahannock Station. When we arrived on the next morning the enemy followed close to our rear, battle was offered them this side of the river but they did not accept. On the following morning they attempted to cross a ford a short distance from the station and our division was thrown forward to meet them. Our brigade had the advance and it turned out to be an artillery fight so all we had to do was support a battery. Our cannon repulsed them although we were exposed all day to their artillery fire. Yet, we had but two men wounded and one killed in the 23rd. We remained on field during the night but in the morning we were relieved and sent back to camp tired enough. The next day we marched back to Warrenton. On the next day we marched down to Sulphur Springs (near

79

Centerville) where our division was engaged in another artillery fight all day. This time our company was deployed along the river as skirmishers and for the first time we fired our guns at rebels. For as time seemed to favor us we did not lose a man. We remained on the field during the night and the morning revealed the fact that the enemy had gone.

About noon we began to march back to Warrenton and from there to Gainesville. While on the march I received your last letter and it gave me new strength to endure the hardships to which we were subjected. We marched that night until midnight when we halted until four in the morning and then we moved to Gainesville where we halted until the middle of the afternoon, when we moved towards Bull Run. We had not proceeded very far before the enemy were found to be in the front. About five o'clock the advance brigade became engaged until darkness closed the bloody scene of one of the sharpest conflicts that took place between the infantry that I have ever seen. Our being in the rear most of the day we did not become engaged but one company and another were thrown out as skirmishers on the flanks. Our men drove the enemy from the field, but with heavy losses. General Gibbon's brigade was fearfully cut to pieces. We remained on the field without a wink of sleep until 2 o'clock in the morning when we began to march to Manassas Junction where we arrived about sunrise. Rations were distributed and about noon we began to march back, taking a different road, where we camped upon an enemy flank. The battle had been raging all day and as we came up our forces drove them from their position. We were pushed up to the front. It being dusk, we exchanged a few volleys when the firing ceased. The battery to which Tommy Sanders was transferred was charged upon by the enemy and Tommy was either killed or taken prisoner. It is thought the latter.

Our company was thrown forward as pickets until midnight when we were relieved. The morning showed that the enemy, too, have fallen back and taken new positions. The forenoon was spent in arranging our forces for the attack. About 2 o'clock it began with our division on the right of the center supporting General Porter. We had to make an advance through a piece of woods. The enemy soon opened upon our columns with cannon and infantry. Our forward line rose up and charged forward with cheers. We followed amid the showers of bullets, shells and cannisters, walking around the dead and dying. I wish I could describe the feelings that possess us at such a time. With me, and I think the experience of nearly all, the fear which one feels before the engagement begins is entirely gone and a recklessness takes on and thus it is that men will give cheer after cheer which advancing directly up to the cannons' mouth with their comrades falling thick and fast about them.

We soon found that our position was untenable, the enemy were turning the left flank of our forces and pouring in upon us a terrible enfilading fire, hence we had to pull back. We fell back behind our batteries in a place where the whole field of conflict was in full view. It was the grandest, most terrible scene I ever beheld. They were turning our left. They fought with the desperation of madmen, charging again and again upon our batteries while they were mowed down by grape and cannisters like grass before a scythe. Our let flank fell back to a new position and held them in check. I think the enemy's losses must have been nearly two to one yet it was terrible on our side. Our division marched back to Centerville that night. We rested the next day until five o'clock when our regiment, with another brigade went to Fairfax, guarding a wagon train and supplies. We stayed over night and in the morning we started to march back when we were ordered off to the left on a different road to hold some rifle pits, protecting our right flank. We laid there that night amid a cold rain with a fire to make coffee and keep us warm. We remained there until three o'clock the next afternoon when all the forces but the rear guard had passed. We then started for the old familiar spot, marching fourteen miles to get there (Centerville). The enemy's cavalry followed close in our rear. The enemy was shelling the pickets of our brigade and we are ordered out to reinforce them. No engagement is expected tonight. I have taken a cold and I am going to stick to the rifle pits for the night. We are most heartily glad that "Little Mack" has again been put in supreme command. He is the best general our nation has. At least the army thinks there is no other man. McClellan has again proved himself, while Pope's bombastic order will become sentence of deepest sarcasm turned upon him.

During the retreat some of our knapsacks had to be burned and mine among them. I lost my journal and also my mess kit. We had perfect confidence that we could repulse the enemy at every front here. It is our nation's darkest hour but the darkest hour is just before the dawn. It is the enemy's last desperate struggle. They have accomplished more than we had expected, but they have their whole force in the field and it must decrease fast while ours is constantly augmenting. A trust for different signs in our national horizon within the next few weeks.

As ever,
Seymour

Pope's forces withdrew August 30-31 to Centerville by way of the Warrenton Turnpike to the Fairfax Court House area.

    Seymour expresses his concern for Tommy Sanders, one of his buddies, and for a good reason. Tom had been temporarily assigned to the First New Hampshire Battery; during the height of the battle at Gainesville, his battery was overrun and, in the dark, it was rather difficult to decide which way to get out of the fight, in view of the fact that he was surrounded by Confederate soldiers and he was caught in a crossfire between the rebels and the federals. The logical thing was to give up. Tom was taken prisoner and removed to the rear. At first, the Rebel captain suggested that they shoot him rather than take him prisoner, but he gave it some thought and asked a private to take him away with some other prisoners. Being as dark as it was, the Confederate private taking Tom to the rear started to ask questions and it turned out that the private, by the name of Allison, had known Tom from Huntsville, Alabama. Strange that they should meet again in such a remote spot and under such a condition. As a result, Tom was kindly treated by his captors and sent to Columbus, Ohio, as a prisoner. For prisoner exchange he was released by the Confederates on January 23, 1863, at which time he rejoined his outfit.

    The journal referred to in Seymour's letter, that was seemingly lost, apparently was found and turned up somewhere in his travels, although he made no later reference to it. Tom Sanders' letter to Seymour follows in its entirety, after Col. Nirom Crane's official report to Brigadier-General M.R. Patrick (see pages 90–94). The journal is now in the possession of the Chemung County Historical Society, Elmira, New York.

Rappahannock to Bull Run

Seymour admitted that it would be quite impossible to relate all the events that followed the leaving of Fredericksburg in a letter. There is no doubt that Company K with the 23rd Regiment was constantly on the move from the 10th of August on through to the finale of the Battle of Antietam.

The regiment arrived at Cedar Mountain after the battle but from then on it was one event followed by another beginning with the Battle of Rappahannock Station August 23, 1862, followed by the Battle of Rocky Gap (or White Sulphur Springs), August 26–27, 1862.

It was a forced march from Rocky Gap the evening of the 27th to Warrenton and on to Gainesville, arriving at the early morning hours of the 28th to become engaged with the Confederates at the edge of the highway at Gainesville.

The 23rd embarked on the highway for Manassas Junction at 2 a.m. that morning.

The regiment arrived at Bull Run by way of the Sudley Springs Road circumventing Longstreet's Division which were spread out along the western section of the Bull Run area, from the Warrenton Alexandria Road up to the unfinished railroad where Jackson's troops spread to the north a distance of about three miles to the Sudley Church along the ravines and woods along the railroad.

At this point, prior to the report of Bull Run, a report by Nirom Crane on the battles of Rappahannock Station and Rocky Gap would be in order. These two battles were the beginning of that action Company K had been so apprehensive about for many months.

These two reports along with Gainesville and Bull Run were not made until after the troops had arrived at Upton's Hill.

After the din of battle had ceased, guns cleaned and cannon filled with grape and cannister in preparedness for any event to follow, the 23rd settled back for a few hours of respite. It was at this time that Col. Nirom Crane, in the absence of Col. H.C. Hoffman, filed his following official reports of Rappahannock Station, White Sulphur Springs and the second Battle of Bull Run.

Rappahannock Station

Headquarters 23rd Regiment N.Y.S. Vols. Capt. Kimball, Asst. Adjutant-General 1st. Div. 3d Brig., 1st. A.C.:

Sir, I have the honor to report the part taken by my command in the fight at the ford above Rappahannock Station, on the days of the 21st and 22nd of August.

On the morning of August 21st our artillery opened upon the enemy who appeared at the ford. I received orders to march my command with the brigade to the support of our batteries and prevent the enemy from crossing. I at once proceeded to the point designated, and under orders from General Patrick, took position just in rear of a section of Reynolds' battery, formed in double column closed en masse and protected by a natural embankment upon which the guns were placed. The cannonading at this point was terrific throughout the day. I had four men wounded, two seriously.

I remained in this position about six hours, when it was ascertained that the enemy in some force had effected a crossing at the ford. The brigade was ordered to the bank of the river, to drive back the enemy and prevent the movement. I proceeded with my command to that point and formed in double column close to the bank of the river, somewhat protected from the enemy's sharp-shooters and artillery by a rise of ground in front.

We remained in this position under a severe fire till about dusk, when General Patrick learned that the enemy were planting a battery so as to sweep the ravine in which the brigade lay. He at once gave the order to fall back to the position of the morning. I proceeded immediately to execute the order; and to do so I was compelled to march in double column faced to the rear of a slope of about thirty rods, where the shot and shell from the enemy's artillery were falling very thick. I gave the necessary orders and moved at double quick up the slope and through a thick grove of pine, while a storm of iron rained upon us. One man was cut in two by a solid shot during this movement. That was the only casualty at this point. We took the position occupied in the morning and lay in line of battle all night.

I would here add that this was the first time my regiment had ever been under fire of artillery. I was highly pleased with the conduct of the men. They were cool and prompt to obey orders. Both men and officers behaved like veterans—not a man flinched from his duty.

The next morning our brigade was relieved by General Doubleday's and moved back to camp about eight a.m. While my command was leaving the field it was subjected to a severe fire from the enemy's artillery but no one was injured.

About three o'clock p.m. I was ordered to take my command and proceed to a ford just above the point of attack and guard the same. Upon arriving, I found a brigade of General Banks' corps doing the duty to which I had been assigned. I reported the fact to General Patrick and was ordered back to camp.—N.M. Crane, Lieutenant-Colonel Commanding.

White Sulphur Springs

The next morning we proceeded to White Sulphur Springs. As the head of the column arrived in sight, the enemy opened upon us with artillery. The brigade was formed in line of battle, my command to the left of the Springs and to the left of the brigade. I was ordered to advance up a hill into and through a piece of woods and drive the enemy across the river. I threw forward two companies as skirmishers, Company G, Captain Doty, and Company K, Captain Fowler, and advanced at a double quick as I was exposed to an enfilading fire from the enemy's batteries. I crossed the field and wood and halted my battalion under cover of the wood.

In crossing this field, my horse in attempting to leap a broad ditch, floundered and fell upon me but the yielding nature of the soil saved my limbs and I immediately re-mounted and pressed forward.

The two companies of skirmishers advanced about one hundred and fifty yards to the front, coming to the river, but found no rebels on our side; but their skirmishers were just on the other side and opened fire upon my men, who returned it vigorously. Skirmishing continued for some time and decidedly to our advantage, as a number of the enemy were killed and wounded. We so annoyed the enemy that he placed two pieces "in battery" and opened upon us. At this moment Colonel G.W. Pratt reported to me that he was ordered by General Patrick to my support with his regiment, the Twentieth New York State Militia. The cannonading now became so heavy, and my position was so exposed, that I received orders from General Patrick to fall back about thirty rods to the left and to the shelter of a ravine. I did so, causing the bugle to sound the call, "skirmishers rally on the battalion." The roar of artillery and the crack of rifles prevented my order being heard by Company G, but Company K came in and joined the regiment. The enemy about this time ceased firing and finding Company G still at its post and no one injured, I concluded to let them remain overnight and sent forward two companies—Companies I and E—to take position on the right and left of Company G, to prevent any surprise or flank movement. I rode forward, in person, just at dusk to see the exact situation of affairs and found everything in order.

On the following morning we were ordered to join the brigade, about 1-1/2 miles to the rear. The division was now put on the march for Warrenton, my regiment forming the rear-guard.

Bull Run

This morning (August 30th.), after giving time to get coffee, the brigade changed positions two or three times to different parts of the field. No enemy in force was discovered. Notwithstanding, our batteries kept throwing shell into the woods to draw them out or bring forth a response but all continued silent.

About two p.m. our division was placed under command of Fitz-John Porter, and with his corps, ordered to advance. It was the prevailing opinion that the enemy had retired, having been defeated on the previous day.

We advanced, King's division having the right and forming four lines of battle. My regiment was the third line of the division. (General Hatch was now in command, General King having been relieved for the affair at Gainesville on the 28th.) We now moved forward to a thick wood. Here the skirmishers commenced firing and soon the advanced lines opened with terrific volleys of musketry. We pushed on. Soon the bullets flew around us as thick as hail. Now commenced in earnest the final battle of Bull Run. The enemy's artillery opened upon us with shot and shell and this, with their musketry, made a storm of their fire. Our artillery in rear of the woods could give us no support.

Thus the battle raged for about 1-1/2 hours until our front lines were broken and the dead and wounded lay in heaps. The enemy lay behind a railroad embankment, and so well protected that our men charged in vain upon them, sometimes upon the ditch, and fought hand-to-hand. Sykes' brigade of regulars on our left was forced back, our two front lines were decimated and broken, and our (Patrick's) brigade badly cut to pieces. Colonel Pratt, of the Twentieth New York State Militia, was killed and the regiment scattered and demoralized. The Twenty-first was used up and the left wing of the Thirty-fifth decimated. These had all left the field and fallen back.

I had heard no orders to retire, and remained in the woods some little time, my regiment being almost alone. I finally gave the orders to retire (right of companies to the rear), and did so in as perfect order as on battalion drill. (In this action I lost a number of men and officers wounded, but only a few killed. Providence has thus far seemed to favor us.)

On emerging from the woods I met General Patrick and saw at once that the battle was going against us, as the enemy had turned our left and the fighting was terrific of musketry and artillery on that part of the field. Our brigade was got together (what was left) and we took a position in rear of a battery, and the men ordered to lie down.

We lay in this position about half an hour, then were ordered toward the rear and left. As we moved over the field the enemy continued to throw shot and shell at us; but fortunately none of my regiment were hit. As we came out upon the pike, General McDowell rode up, his horse all covered with foam and dust, and he, himself, looking nearly exhausted with fatigue and excitement and ordered us toward Centreville. We continued the March and soon learned that the army were on the retreat to Washington.

We arrived at Centreville about ten p.m., worn out and exhausted. We lay down upon the ground so completely tired that we did not mind the rain that commenced, but slept soundly till morning and wet to the skin.

As I awoke in the morning and realized the situation of affairs, and that we had left our dead and wounded in the hands of the enemy, thoughts of the sufferings of those noble heroes left behind with no comrades near to stanch the bleeding wound— who must lay perhaps for days (as they did) without food—to give life or water to quench their burning thirst, thus to suffer a thousand deaths, the thought was agonizing in the extreme, and I could not keep back the blinding tears, and it filled my heart too full for utterance. Thank God none of my regiment were left behind.

Then, again, our country! Our army in full retreat, hotly pressed on our flank and rear by a strong and merciless foe flushed with victory, within thirty miles of our capitol, and confidence in our generals lost, this was enough to demoralize the entire army. No recollections of my short life could bring up an hour of such utter dejection and despondency. I felt as though all was lost.

It was about nine a.m. when we received the news that General McClellan was again in command of the army of the Potomac. The effect was wonderful and thrilling. For miles along the lines of that battle-shattered and disheartened army cheer upon cheer rent the air, and the sound swelled and rolled along like a wave. Officers sprang into their saddles with a bound, soldiers grasped their muskets with eagerness and sprang to their places in the ranks, and at the order forward, all moved as if invigorated with renewed life. We all felt that we were again a host and could and would save our Capitol and country.

We marched on toward Fairfax two or three miles and halted near the road. About five p.m. my regiment and the Twenty-first New York were ordered to proceed to Fairfax for the purpose of guarding a wagon-train to that place. We did so, and when within about one mile of our destination the enemy attacked the train but only succeeded in killing one mule and then retired, satisfied

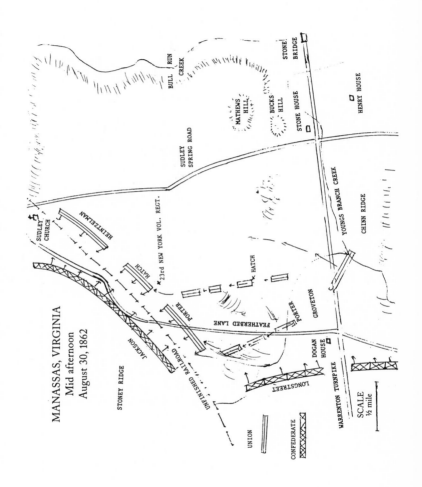

MANASSAS, VIRGINIA
Mid afternoon
August 30, 1862

SCALE
½ mile

UNION
CONFEDERATE

that the experiment would not prove profitable. It commenced raining and we concluded to remain all night at Fairfax.

The next morning we commenced our return toward Centreville and had proceeded about 2-1/2 miles when we met the balance of the brigade and countermarched. About this time we learned that the enemy were about to make an attack at a point near Chantilly. Our brigade was moved in that direction and the Thirty-fifth, Twenty-first and Twenty-third were placed in an old rebel rifle-pit to protect the right of our line of battle. About sundown the enemy attacked our left and the battle lasted till about nine p.m. The firing of musketry and artillery was incessant, and this, with the terrific thunder and lightning, rendered the scene grand and terrible. The enemy were repulsed with considerable loss. We remained here until the following afternoon, when we were ordered to march for Upton's Hill. We set out immediately and reached that place about midnight.

End of Report

Col. Hoffman had become ill on June 1, but continued to keep up with the regiment. He had not fully recovered from his illness and just prior to Cedar Mountain and Bull Run, Gen. King ordered him to Washington for recuperation. He did go to Bailey's Cross Roads to Mrs. Bailey's house for rest. Col. Hoffman confided in a letter to his brother, while there, that officers are not supposed to get sick. Lt. Col. Crane had taken over as acting commander of the regiment.

Referring to the 800 men of Gibbon's Brigade at Gainesville: "What shall be said in honor of such men? Who can face death by the hour, a little band against a swarm? Who could steadily reload their pieces and send death into that swarm while cannon belched iron hail into their faces, while musketry threw a storm of lead at them? Their brave officers taken one by one and their brave comrades fell around them like sheaves full ripe before the avenging scythe of death, still they did not falter. 800 men died in seventy minutes. What a glorious tribute to men who fight for a cause"—Quote from William Maxson's Campfires of the 23rd.

Gibbon's Brigade had been on the go for several days. This particular day they had engaged the enemy after a long morning

Opposite: Map showing position of 23rd New York Volunteer Regiment at Manassas, Virginia, mid afternoon, August 30, 1862.

and six miles' marching in the heat with no breakfast. They certainly deserve credit for their tenacity in the face of death, under adverse conditions brought about by the fortunes of war.

Tommy Sanders' letter to Seymour while a Confederate prisoner:

Columbus, Ohio
Sept. 21, 1862

Dear Friend:

Thinking that perhaps you might like to know that I am still in the land of the living, and being myself anxious to know what has befallen you amid the turmoil of the last few weeks, I take this method of opening communication with you, though I fear the answer will contain sad news. To tell who is living and who dead in these times is indeed difficult; but I am happy to tell you (as you doubtless mistrust ere you have read thus far) that I am all right and I earnestly hope that you also are in the same condition. The most that I dare hope for is that you are alive and able to tote your knapsack through the day, that you are not aroused more than three times a night to receive the rebs who have no intention of visiting you, and that your teeth are in proper order to consume your ration of Uncle Sam's pies. Happiness beyond this is not to be expected in the army.

I am at present situated in one of the most pleasant spots in this good State of Ohio, am living on the top shelf, enjoying the pleasures of civilization. Were I to tell you of my very kind and agreeable friends, Mr. and Mrs. Crawford, whose hospitality I am sharing, of their splendid residence, and of my pleasant room in it, of apples, peaches, pears, cider and high living generally, it might make you discontented. To tantalize you with accounts of oyster suppers, dances, rides and visits with the fair ones of Columbus, would be the last degree of cruelty. I sometimes wish the rebs had left me in Virginia, when I think of leaving all this and returning to the army, as I shall probably do very soon. Then, some evening as we sit beside the campfire I will spin out the particulars of my sojourn here.

Perhaps you would like to know something of my adventures

before reaching Ohio. My experiences in Rebeldom and journey thence were not very agreeable.

We went into the fight, I suppose, about the time that you did. We kept the Gainesville Turnpike till we crossed the brook and passed a little old house on the left of the road and on the side of a hill. On the top of this hill we went into battery under a pretty sharp fire. Doubleday's brigade went in on our left. The rebel fire continued to increase till it became a perfect storm. The infantry had scarcely formed when they broke and went down the hill pell-mell. They made a partial rally at the foot and again commenced the ascent, but had not reached the top when they gave way a second time, and that is the last I have seen of them. In the meantime, we kept up our thunder to the best of our ability. While our cannister lasted we swept them off terribly but we had only ten rounds to the gun, as the caissons were left in the rear. After cannister was played out they had a decided advantage of us, as they were so near that we could do nothing with shell and shrapnel. They came on, howling in the most approved Secesh style, I should judge—at least I never heard such noises from human beings. Our men who had fallen back were pouring their fire into us and the rebs were doing likewise. In short, things were getting pretty badly mixed. They were soon upon us. By the aid of darkness all the guns managed to get off but one, which had recoiled into a gutter, so that we could not limber up in the short time allowed us. The first thing I knew of the actual presence of the rebs, one who was foremost in the charge came up to me with his bayonet pointed for my breast and very fiercely demanded: "What regiment do you belong to?"

I was in my shirtsleeves and had on a citizen's hat, so he could not tell whether I was Secesh or Yankee. I answered him in genuine Yankee style by asking: "What regiment do you belong to? "Fourth Alabama!" said he.

I left him without further conversation, thinking that I could get to our men. I don't know whether the fellow shot at me or not, as there were so many bullets hissing around. When I reached the brook I saw that a whole regiment of rebs had crossed before me. To go through them and to our army, when both were firing, was too much of an undertaking for me, so I sat down and concluded to take it cool. It was not many minutes before a reb came along and asked: "Are you wounded?" "Not very bad!" I said. "What regiment do you belong to?" he asked. "First New Hampshire battery!" I said, thinking it no longer of any use to play off. "Get up and come along, then!" said he, adding a few oaths by way of emphasis. I stood up. "Have you got any weapons about you?" he asked. "No!" I answered. "Any knives?" "No!" "Anything in your pockets?" "No!"

About this time he very unceremoniously took my hat off my head, putting his in its place, saying, "he reckoned he'd trade hats with me." As we approached his regiment he began to halloo to his comrades very exultingly, saying he had got one of the d——d Yankees who had been shooting at them. He took me to his captain, telling him he had captured a d——d Yankee. "I don't want him! D——n him! Kill him!" said the captain. They d——d me off in grand style. The fellow drew his gun ready to pierce me, and I really began to think that they did mean to kill me. Finally the captain said: "Somebody take him to the rear!"

A fellow who was standing by said his gun was so dirty that he could do nothing with it, and he would take me. So, we started for the rear. The firing had ceased for a few minutes, but it commenced again with redoubled fury. After a short talk with the chap who was taking me to the rear, we were both very much surprised to find that we were old acquaintances. I had known him several years ago in Huntsville, Ala. Although a strange meeting for friends, we were friends nevertheless. As soon as we were out of reach of bullets we sat down and had a long talk of old times, the people of Huntsville, war, politics, etc., etc. Among other interesting items, he told me that all my lady acquaintances of that place were married, and that my favorite one had been the cause of a shooting affair between two gentlemen, in which one was killed. The conqueror, of course, won the prize. To say the least, I am happy that I am not in the place of the one who was killed.

After talking over matters of most interest we found that it was getting late in the evening and I was beginning to shiver with cold. All had become quiet in front, so my friend (Allison) suggested that if we should go back to the battlefield, I could pick up a blanket, which I very much needed, as all my clothing was on the limber of the gun which I could not get to then. We went back to the field and I was not long in finding a blanket. It is no use to tell you of the sights we saw there, of dead, dying and mangled men. My friend's comrade had been killed by our cannon and he was feeling very sad. What a war! Friends, and even brothers, are killing each other.

Allison said he must see his captain before going back with me (he had agreed to stay with me that night), but he did not wish to take me to the front, as they might commence firing again. I told him that

Camp scene, 23rd Regiment, Company C, unidentified soldiers (courtesy National Archives).

I would go with him. We found his regiment lying down on the next hill beyond the brook with guns all ready for something to come over the hill. I found a whole company from Huntsville and had quite a talk with them. They were very much elated with their success and were sure of having Washington in a few days. Allison had a talk with his captain and we started to the rear again. After traveling about three miles we came to where a squad of prisoners were sleeping under guard. Here we lay down and slept till morning. On awaking, I found our captain and eight of the battery boys in the squad. Allison said that he must go to his regiment—so we shook hands, hoping, if we ever met again, it would not be with weapons in our hands trying to kill each other.

That morning we were marched to Gainesville, where we were

kept till the next Monday at noon (this was Sunday). They gave us nothing to eat for the very good reason that they had nothing to give. But, they treated us kindly. They seemed to be a band of brothers, all striving for the same object and all in earnest—a great deal more so than our army. They were badly clothed and scantily fed, yet there was no complaining. On Sunday, three hundred out of our crowd started on their march for Harpers Ferry. Monday, at noon, the rest of us (1,200) commenced our march for the Point of Rocks, where we arrived the next Wednesday.

No one can appreciate our experience at Gainesville, or our march from there, till they have been through something similar. We went into the fight on Friday night hungry and worn out—from then till Monday they gave us nothing to eat. On our march to the Point of Rocks we lived on green corn. Most of the boys had no blanket, and some, like myself, had no jacket. We lay out in all the storms which succeeded the battle, in that condition, without the protection of tents. At the Point of Rocks, an Ohio regiment which was stationed there, turned over to us all their rations and the cheering, patriotic words and noble conduct of their colonel did us almost as much good as the eatables. It was indeed pleasing to see the stars and stripes again, and to be among friends.

From the Point of Rocks we went on the Baltimore and Ohio road to Cumberland, where we staid about a week and were treated with much kindness by the inhabitants. From there we went through by rail to Columbus. No soldier in that party will ever cease to be grateful to the Ohio ladies for their kindness as we passed through their villages. Most of us had no money—in fact, we needed none. At all the places where the train stopped for any length of time, hundreds of ladies would be on the platforms with baskets of eatables, smiles and cheering words for us. I heard many a "God bless them" come from the roughest of characters, showing that a soft spot somewhere under their jackets had been touched.

But I have spun this out too long already. Hoping that I shall very soon hear that you are all right, I remain your friend and comrade,

T.C.S.

When the battery of the 1st New Hampshire artillery was over-run at Groveton, Virginia, two men were killed and several

men wounded. Capt. George A. Gerrish, who commanded the battery along with eight other men, and Tommy Sanders were captured.

Capt. Gerrish was released at once on an exchange; the enlisted men were taken into Ohio. Tommy Sanders was released the following January (1863) and returned to Company K at Belle Plains, Virginia.

Capt. Gerrish rejoined his New Hampshire artillery unit, which served under General Hooker's command at Antietam, Fredericksburg, Chancellorsville, Gettysburg, the Wilderness, Spotsylvania, Cold Harbor and Petersburg, and which finally cooled its guns at Appomattox.

The Battles of South Mountain and Antietam

After Bull Run, the 23rd needed and received a couple of weeks respite from the rigors of travel and constant movement to say nothing of Bull Run. The vacation was short lived. The regiment was ordered to proceed north through Maryland. After seven days of marching, the regiment settled for the night on the south bank of the Monocacy River opposite Frederick. Col. Hoffman joined the regiment on the march although he did so against the advice of the physician.

It was not long before the Union troops covered the valley of Middletown, east of South Mountain. The troops halted for dinner on the afternoon of the 14th after advancing close to the base of South Mountain earlier in the day. About 3 p.m. they formed a battle line close to the Stone Church at Turner's Gap.

Briefly, Col. Hoffman's report of the battles of South Mountain and Antietam follows.

South Mountain Sept. 14, 1862

Headquarters 23rd Regiment
New York Vol.
Near Sharpsburg, Maryland
Sept. 20, 1862

Brig. Gen. M. R. Patrick:

In compliance with orders, I respectfully submit the following report of the part taken by my command in the engagement at "South

Mountain," near Middletown, Washington County, Md., on Sunday the 14th day of September, 1862:

We left Frederick with brigade about eight o'clock a.m., and proceeded on the old government turnpike through the village of Middletown to near the foot of South Mountain, where we rested one hour for refreshments and again moved forward with the brigade to the right of the turnpike and along the foot of the mountain, under cover of a hill and out of range of the enemy's guns then in position on the top of the mountain, a distance of about half a mile. At this point we were ordered to support the Thirty-fifth Regiment, New York Vol., whose entire line was thrown forward as skirmishers and ascending the hill, their left resting on the turnpike and extending to the right a full half mile.

We advanced in line of battle in close sustaining distance of the skirmishers about half-way up the mountain side to a lane, where we unslung knapsacks which had become cumbersome, owing to the rough and rocky plowed fields over which we had passed and the fences we had climbed.

From this point we marched obliquely to the left until our left rested within about 300 yards of the gorge and mountain through which the old government turnpike passes, and advanced with the skirmishers in this position until nearly to the top of the mountain and into the woods where we halted and remained in position about fifteen minutes, when I moved my right wing, by your order, one fourth of a mile to the right in support of the right wing of the line of skirmishers of the 35th, leaving the left wing in command of Lt.-Col. N.M. Crane.

On arriving at the right I found Hatch's brigade, under command of Col. Phelps, advancing in line of battle immediately behind me and in supporting distance of the line of skirmishers, whereupon I immediately, and without orders, moved my right wing back to join my left, knowing that flank to be but feebly supported.

We then advanced in line following the skirmishers in an oblique direction to the right along the slope of the mountain, over a very rocky bottom, our left all the time at from 200 to 400 yards from the turnpike and near the cleared field, until the main line had reached the top of the mountain, and was engaged on the right, when by your order removed by the right flank up the side of the gorge to the support of the left of the line of Hatch's brigade, which by this time (dark) had become hotly engaged with the enemy's infantry.

We remained in this position 15 minutes, by which time it had become quite dark, and were then ordered by you into a position in the line of fire, which had grown very weak and was likely to give way, when we advanced to the fence and opened fire through the corn field upon the enemy.

After delivering our fire of about twelve rounds, the enemy's fire nearly ceased and we were ordered to cease firing, which we did, and corrected our alignment about three yards back of the fence, when we were ordered by you to move off the field with you and a portion of the 23rd which had been assembled at that point. At this time it was very dark and everything in confusion, and upon starting from the field the enemy opened a brisk fire again. We were now ordered, by an aid of General Doubleday, to advance again to the fence.

We did so, and commenced firing, but after delivering a few rounds were again ordered to cease firing, which we did, and undertook to form a line again when a brigade came up in the darkness hooting and yelling, running over everybody and throwing everything into even worse confusion than before. It finally terminated in a general mob, rendering it impossible for any line to be kept in order.

The enemy's fire had, however, ceased and after an hour and a half, when the battle had been won and all was quiet, I assorted my command from the jam, rallied it on the colors, and we groped our way back to the place where we had left our knapsacks on the hillside, arriving at about eleven o'clock p.m. Here we found the 35th regiment going into camp for the night. All the men were found present at reveille the next morning, except those disabled in the action.

In this engagement the officers and men of my command behaved in a manner highly creditable to themselves. Next morning, (September 15th) we rendezvoused with the brigade at the turnpike, and we proceeded with it toward Boonsboro.

In this action we had but nine companies (Company C being on duty at division headquarters), consisting of three field, one staff and fifteen line officers, and one hundred and eighty-three enlisted men.

H.C. Hoffman
Colonel Commanding

Antietam Sept. 17, 1862

> Headquarters 23rd Regiment
> New York Vol.
> Near Sharpsburg, Md.
> Sept. 20, 1862

Brigadier-General M.R. Patrick:

I hereby respectfully submit the following report of the part taken by my command in the battle of Sharpsburg, or Antietam, fought September 17th, 1862.

After the battle of South Mountain, near Middletown, Maryland, fought on Sunday evening, September 14th, 1862, we marched with the brigade, on the morning of the 15th of September, to a point near Keedysville and encamped for the night.

We proceeded next morning (Sept. 16th) to a point near Sharpsburg and occupied the day in changing position from one point on the field to another until almost evening, when we were marched across the Antietam Creek and took our position amid a tremendous fire of artillery from the enemy on the extreme right of the entire army. By this time it was dark and we lay on our arms all night.

At early dawn on the morning of the 17th, the enemy opened a fire of artillery on us, under which we lay for about three-quarters of an hour, when we were moved with the rest of the brigade to the left about half a mile and in range of the enemy's guns to the support, as I understood, of General Gibbon's brigade, which was, at that time, hotly engaged with the enemy's forces with artillery and small-arms and advanced up in the rear of Campbell's battery and from thence moved to the right by a flank movement, and halted in the edge of the woods, the left of the column resting on the turnpike leading to Sharpsburg. Here I was ordered to move with my command to the right of the line to reconnoiter and watch the movement of a large body of the enemy who were reported to be gaining our right flank and rear, but had proceeded only a short distance when the order was countermanded, and I was sent back to join the brigade, by order of General Doubleday, a regiment having been detached from another brigade to perform the duty assigned to my command.

We then marched back by the left flank at double quick and joined our brigade just in time to advance with it to the ledge of rocks on the right and in front of Campbell's regular battery, and opened fire on the flank column of the enemy which was advancing through the cornfield and on the battery, driving them back in great haste and with much slaughter.

We, with the brigade, were after the fleeing rebels across the clover field to the turnpike and remained there a short time delivering a heavy fire into the enemy, when suddenly the discovery was made that our brigade was flanked on the right by the enemy in large force, and, by your direction, we fell back in perfect order to the ledge of rocks where we halted and stopped the advancing foe.

By this time our ammunition had nearly given out, and upon re-inforcements coming up we fell back a short distance behind a rise of ground, stacked arms, and were preparing to make coffee when a rebel battery, suddenly brought into position on our right, opened fire and was getting range on us. We then moved forward into the woods and lay under a heavy fire of artillery about half an hour when three lines of our infantry, said to be Sedgwick's Division, entered the woods on our left, but were soon driven back in great disorder, making much confusion among all troops in that vicinity; but I succeeded in keeping the ranks in order and moving up to the ledge of rocks before mentioned, where it was impossible to deliver a fire without endangering our own fleeing men.

At the same time, the enemy poured a brisk fire into our right flank and rear, when we were ordered by you to return which was done in such perfect order as to elicit the notice and highly complimentary and flattering remarks of Brigadier-General Howard, in addressing his own flying men whom he was nobly but vainly attempting to rally.

That brave soldier pointed to us as an example for the disorganized saying as he did so: "Men! that is the way to leave a field. That regiment are acting like soldiers! Do as they do men and we will drive them back again in ten minutes."

We retired to the edge of the woods, immediately back of the point where Campbell's battery was situated, and formed with the rest of the brigade along the fence and succeeded with the assistance of other troops, who were rallied in our rear and on our right, in presenting such a front as to intimidate the enemy from any further advance. After remaining in this position until order was again restored we were relieved by other troops and were moved off to the rear, replenished our ammunition, and lay in support of the regular line of batteries until night.

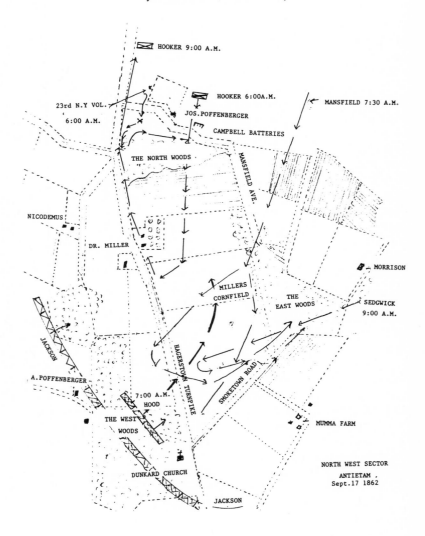

Map showing position of 23rd New York Volunteer Regiment at Antietam, Virginia, Northwest Sector, September 17, 1862.

There was no infantry fight on our front after we left the field. We had but eight companies in this battle, Company C having been detached some days previous for duty at division headquarters and being with the train, and Company B being on picket duty on the right and in front of our position in the morning and on the night before.

The officers and men of my command who went into the action behaved most admirably, never deranging their alignment during the surgings back and forward of the lines, obeying with promptitude every order, and all the time remaining firm, steady, and never moving until they had received the full order.

Their conduct was all that I could wish. We had one field, one staff, thirteen line officers, and 223 enlisted men. Our casualties were four killed and thirty-five wounded.

H.C. Hoffman
Colonel Commanding

President Lincoln, in his talks with General McClellan, questioned him in reference to the mounting absenteeism among his troops. The Federals were plagued by sickness in the camps and many of the injured had been sent home to recuperate. The theory behind home recuperation was that the therapy of home care far exceeded the ability of the camp hospitals to cope with the innumerable cases of injured and ill. It was hopeful that home care would speed up the recovery and return of the troops to the field. Unfortunately, this was not the case and, as it so happened, it was estimated that in 1861 and 1862 no more than ten percent of the home care cases returned to active duty.

In a review of the Maryland Campaign of 1862 by General James Longstreet in his book, From Manassas to Appomattox, *General Longstreet had been rebuked by President Jeff Davis for the same problem. Longstreet, in his reply to Jeff Davis, said that unjust criticism has been passed upon the Confederate soldiers in the Maryland campaign, based principally upon the great number of absentees: "To those who have spent their lives near the ranks of soldiers and learned from experience that there is a limit of physical endurance, explanation is not called for; to those who look upon the soldier as a machine not even needing oil to facilitate motive power, I will say, try*

1st Sgt. Duane Thompson, 23rd Regiment, Company K (courtesy National Archives).

to put yourself in the soldier's place. Another point to be noted was that in the Confederate ranks were thousands of soldiers who had been wounded twice and, in some instances, three times, who in any other service would have been on the pension rolls at their comfortable homes.

Sickness and weakness that creep into an army from irregular food collected in the stress of march were no trifling impediments to the maintenance of our ranks in vigorous forms."

The northern drive of General Lee which had hoped to continue at the time into the north of Maryland and Pennsylvania had been secondarily motivated by the fact that the South badly needed clothing for the soldiers. The supplies of shoes and warmer clothing were needed to augment the rapidly dwindling stock. In fact, many a Southern soldier went to Antietam shoeless.

The invasion force of the Confederacy had been reduced from 100,000 strong to close to 70,000 men fit for duty. Fatigue, disease and stragglers accounted for nearly 30,000 men. General Lee, in one of his reports following his invasion of the North, commented, "The arduous services in which our troops had been engaged, their great privations of rest and food, and the long marches without shoes, had greatly reduced our ranks. These causes had compelled thousands of brave men to absent them- selves and many more had done so through unworthy motives." All the roads of northern Virginia were lined with soldiers— so-called stragglers, but a great majority of these men had fallen out from their ranks because of the physical impossibility of keep- ing up with the rest of the men. Many men did so because the lack of shoes caused severe bleeding of the feet that could just not carry them any farther.

When General Lee and General Jackson moved into Mary- land they hoped to rally the people to the cause of the rebellion but failed to realize that the ragged condition of the troops would turn public sentiment against them.

> Near Sharpsburg, Md.
> Sept. 22, 1862

Mailed from Hagerstown, Md. (9-25-62)
My Dear Friend:

I embrace the first opportunity that presents itself to me since the late fatigues and battles to write you a short note. Again, all the Alfred boys have been spared and are now enjoying good health except Chapin who is in the hospital at Washington, but not seriously ill.

No doubt you have already received full reports covering the move- ments here in Maryland and also of the late battles, hence it would be idle for me to attempt to give a description even in the space of a sin- gle letter. Suffice it to say we left Upton Hill on the night of the 6th and once more came to this side of the Potomac and began our march toward the enemy then in the vicinity of Frederick. Confidence and order had again been restored to the army. With Gen. George McClel- lan at their head they were not afraid to meet the enemy at any place. On the 12th and 13th the advanced forces under Burnside had skir- mishes with the rear guard of the enemy, but on the 14th they made a stand on South Mountain. The results you already know. McDowell's elite corps de army is spoken of in the highest terms for its gallant con- duct. The losses of our division were very light in that fight and

Patriotic envelopes addressed to Ellenoir Weaver from Seymour Dexter (Camp Diven Stationery).

especially that of our regiment. The 23rd lost none killed, but a few were wounded. Their next stand in which the division was engaged was at Sharpsburg. We were in Hooker's command. On the night before the great battle our division was among the first that crossed the Antietam Creek and passed around so as to threaten the enemy's left flank. The Pa. Vol. Regt. joined us on the left. Just as twilight began to gather around, they found the enemy. The Bucktails engaged them first. Batteries opened up on both sides at close range. It was the grandest artillery firing I ever saw. Although there was firing the next day that exceeded it four-fold in magnitude. Yet, the darkness gave to it a wildness and grandeur that I never saw before. We did picket duty on the extreme right of our lines. That night there was firing somewhere along the lines almost incessantly during the night and at 5 o'clock in the morning the battle began to rage in earnest. It did not cease for a moment until darkness threw down her veil of gloom between the opposing forces. Our division lost heavily but drove the enemy before them. Our brigade repulsed a charge made by the first Texas brigade, taking their colors and many prisoners. The 23rd, in fact, our whole brigade, were extremely fortunate, again. The losses in our regiment were five killed and about 20 wounded. I was reported among the slightly wounded. It was caused by a spent cannon shot striking me just above the right ankle in a glancing manner, bruising it badly and making me quite lame, but I continued with the regiment during the day. We lay upon our arms during the night expecting that daylight would again renew the bloody contest but it did not. Both parties seemed willing to leave in peace. We had possession of nearly the whole battle field, hence our wounded were cared for and many of our dead buried. The scene on the field of conflict is beyond description. In many places the rebel dead were so thick that it seemed as though a battalion had laid down and never risen up. Preparations were made to renew the scene on Friday morning, but the enemy left during the night, their dead unburied and many wounded, uncared for men. We moved down about midway between the field and river and bivouacked. Here we still remain. During the battle McClellan was around and supervising in person. Whenever he came he was always greeted with enthusiastic cheers. Napoleon never was more dearly loved by his soldiers than McClellan is by the volunteers under his command.

There has been cannonading up and down the river almost daily but the results we still do not know.

We feel that a death blow has been given the rebel army of Virginia. They have found that they are not invincible, but I will not speculate as to the future. Time is the only revelator, but I trust that this terrible and wholesale bloodshed may soon cease. We have regiments in our division that cannot now muster 100 men fit for duty out of the original regiment.

I fear my letter is a poor affair, there have been so many deep impressions the past few days. I feel that every attempt to write letters has been a failure. Just received orders to get ready to move so I must close.

> Your true friend,
> Seymour

> Camp Patten
> Near Sharpsburg
> Oct. 12, 1862

Mailed in Washington D.C.
Dear Ellie:

Sunday morning inspection is over with and there are no more duties until dress parade, unless the order to march comes.

A somewhat chilly wind sweeps gently over the hill and dale reminding me of what is fast approaching. The surrounding forests are fast putting on their varied yet beautiful autumnal tints and almost unconsciously one looks about to see the ripened apples and other fruits of the farms, but no such are to be seen here. This section was rich in products four weeks ago but now looks barren and desolate. We still remain camped between Sharpsburg and the river near the battlefield, but we don't expect to remain much longer. We are again under order to be ready at half hours notice.

The battle field still continues to attract large numbers of visitors, some through curiosity, while many come to seek the name of some beloved ones from among the many hundred headboards that mark the resting places of so many and martyrs to the cause of freedom, justice and our union. Our men were buried in single graves with headboards giving their names and regiment but the rebels were simply put in trenches and covered over.

When the army came to a halt here, the enemy having been driven across the river, it was badly used up. A brigade was but a regiment and divisions but brigades, but it has been and is fast being recruited to strength and power again. New regiments have been put in old brigades, thus increasing their efficiency.

New clothing has been issued so the men once more present a respectable appearance for soldiers. Time has dragged somewhat heavily, there being nothing to do. No reading matter is to be obtained except newspapers which we have learned by experience to respect little more rather than camp rumors.

During the recent battles the 23rd was in General Patrick's brigade. General Doubleday's division and General Hooker's Corp. army.

True friend
Seymour

Warrenton, Va.
Nov. 7, 1862

Dear Friend:

I am sitting beneath my shelter tent with a bright fire in front of me, just outside the village of Warrenton, while a regular old northeaster is whirling the first snow flakes of the season around in wild profusion. One week ago Sunday the order forward march once more was spoken to the army of the Potomac. It came to us in the middle of a dismal autumnal storm. It was the first we have experienced, but it soon cleared up and we had most beautiful weather until the present storm, which now promises to be snow instead of rain. We were camped at Bakersville, Md., about midway between Sharpsburg and Williamsport, when we received the word to march. We marched down to Berlin, by way of Cramptons Gap, where we have once more crossed the soil of the Old Dominion on the evening of the 30th. It was a humiliating thought to think that fifteen months before we had crossed the same river for the same purpose and after thirteen months we have been forced back by the foe whom we thought we so speedily reduced but we cross now with high hopes and renewed confidence. So, it was with gay spirits that we ascended the bluffs that border the river and passed on beyond Lovettsville before we halted for the night. On the following day we moved forward only about one mile but on the next day, the first of Nov., we moved forward about 8 miles and pitched our

Pvt. Thomas Sanders, Company K, 23rd New York Volunteer Regiment (courtesy Alfred Academy Archives).

tents in a beautiful place near Purcelleville. Our advance cavalry drove the enemy from that vicinity. While we were coming up, the sound of their light artillery furnished us music to march to. We remained at this place until Sunday but the advance forces were skirmishing with the enemy nearly all day and while we were singing during church exercises. I imagined the roar of the distant cannon formed a bass to the music, the enemy continued to fall back and on Monday we moved about 6 miles farther in the direction of Ashby's Gap and on Tuesday we proceeded to Bloomingdale and on the following day we turned our line of march toward Warrenton and after two days, marching, we arrived here. We must have marched at least 60 miles the last three days.

The retreating rebels left the place a short time before our advanced regiment, the Bucktails, entered it. The town is deserted except for what seems to be a hospital. All public buildings are used as such. When we shall take up our line of march again or in what direction it will be is more than I can tell.

I wish those northern editors, who have been striving to poison the public mind against McClellan, had to sit in my present position to write their infamous editorials. I think they would be much shorter and fewer than at present. Do not understand me to speak like one discouraged. No one is better pleased than myself with this advance, but human endurance has its bounds even in this soldier and they have been far overstepped by northern civilians when talking about a winter campaign. Our movements in the future most necessarily depend much upon the weather. My term of enlistment is only six months longer and I trust that our country will no longer need our services at that time. I long once more to return to civilized life and be removed from the terrible influences that necessarily surround a soldier.

Seymour

Ironically, November 7 was the day that Gen. McClellan received word from President Lincoln that he had been relieved of his command. He reviewed the troops on the 10th and bade them farewell. It was truly a sad day for the 23rd as the "Little Mac" left his heart with the troops that respected and admired him.

On November 11, the 23rd moved in full marching gear toward Fredericksburg. The journey south was marked with the usual heavy rains that made roads impassable, and swamped the artillery and baggage trains. The rain pelted them for three long, miserable days and nights. This made clothes and knapsacks heavy, to say nothing of the four inches of snow that greeted them the first week of December.

Fredericksburg: December 1862

Brooks Station
Stafford Co., Va
Dec. 3, 1862

(Mailed from Washington City Dec. 8, 1862)
(Apparently winter quarters)

I am seated in what we call a "Royal Palace," you may think we have a queer notice of that term when I tell you that our "Palace" is somewhat less than 6 feet square and accommodates three persons— myself, Lewis Kenyon and William Maxson. It is built up of logs about three feet and then our shelter tents put on for a roof. We have a nice fireplace on one side, built in true Virginia style. The chimney is outside. But, let him who thinks our use of the term is not correct live in nothing but a tent a few days with the cold December winds sweeping around and into it by day, and night creeping more searchingly beneath his scanty blankets, and he will decide in our favor. We are at present camped upon a gentle hillside overlooking the railroad near Brooks Station. Almost hourly the scream of the locomotive is echoed from the hill as it hurries with huge trains of commissary and forage supplies. How long we will remain here is uncertain. There are many surmises afloat but the most probable one to me is that Burnside intends to give the enemy battle. They are now fortifying upon the other side of the river. Stretched along the road for a distance of eight miles is a canvas city containing more able bodied men than the great Metropolis. Every loyal state and every caste of society is here represented in this conservator of our nation's power, its honor, its rights and supremacy. Patriotism is one of the noblest and purest emotions that finds habitation in the human breast, its main spring of action and the band of the Union.

Burnside has the confidence of the army but not his love which was bestowed upon McClellan and could the men express their opinion unitedly they would speak in thundertones—"Restore to us 'Little Mac'." The health of the troops is very good, in fact, never better while hopeful spirits generally prevail. I believe the opening of the coming contest will be heard with joy. Joy, not because they love to fight, but because they wish the dreaded inevitable and they think in some measure decisive conflict to be over.

Seymour

Battle of Fredericksburg

At twelve M., on Tuesday, December 9th, we broke camp, very reluctantly, and moved to within the vicinity of Camp "Rufus King," and on the following day (10th) beyond it, and bivouacked in a beautiful grove of pine. The forces were now massed in order and the pontoon bridges ready to be thrown down. The fight opened on the 11th. As the following letter contains the gist of the fight and of the part taken in it by the Twenty-third, we take the liberty to copy. —Written by William Maxson

Letter from William Maxson:

Camp "Paul" (Nowhere),
December 21st, 1862

Dear M---:

On the night before the bombardment we bivouacked in a dense thicket of pines near the old campground known as "Rufus King." We were not long in gathering the cedar boughs, always abundant, and spreading this bed of down over the floor of our little tents. As darkness came on, the huge campfires gave a charming outline and feature to this little fairy city of white roofs. Their bright light in long diverging rays beat back the dark and showed in relief the graceful tapering trunks of the pines, gray and dusky. Their boughs arch and form deep, dark aisles of nature's grand old cathedral filled with dim and spectral shadows. Around the fires groups of hardy soldiers were telling stories.

Aside from the deep, wild interest of battle, the shock of armies when death is wantonly swooping into the gulf of ruin so many precious lives, there is a peculiar something in camp life that may challenge comparison in interest to any other. Take the scene above. This noble band of men have come together to defend liberty with their lives and a cord of sympathy ties the knot around the cheerful campfires. The rude jesting of these great hearts together, as they talk of their mutual dangers, hairbreadth escapes, noble deeds of comrades and the sacred cause, unites them one in purpose, one in action. To be sure, there is a lack of polish of manner and speech about all this (camp dialect is blunt), but it has the plain outspoken manhood, a smack of truth and honor, that atones for much of refinement. We are compelled to look upon it in this light. Such thoughts are born of such a life, no matter how uncultivated the soldier or rude the thought.

The pontoon bridges had been pushed nearly to the opposite shore under cover of darkness, and ere the faintest ray of dawn had streaked the east, the quick, sharp rattle of musketry broke the stillness. The engineers laying the last plank were charged upon and a bloody struggle followed. Ought not that blood to doom that proud and ancient city? It certainly cries to Heaven for vengeance. A shaft of flame leaps out from the opposite shore, the earth trembles, the air breaks with a deafening roar and a huge shell, with a shriek like a demon, speeds out its errand of destruction. Another followed and another, till the storm of iron crushed through the walls and set the town on fire. All day long the incessant thunder of the bombardment shook the hills and rent the air. Our brigade moved down to the river during the day and awaited orders. When the sun sunk darkly into the smoke of burning, the rebels on the opposite hills looked down upon the wreck of their proud city.

On the following morning the sun strove in vain to dispel the mountains of fog that covered the two armies like a shroud and the mist held the river till after noon. Under this kindly cover we crossed the river. As we reached the level of the plain, a rebel battery opened upon the division while en masse, and with surprising accuracy dropped the shell in our midst, but to very little effect. One man in the regiment was slightly wounded. The advance was thrown briskly forward and a footing for the army obtained. Night now closed in upon the opposing armies and they await the morrow.

The morrow came, and with it the conflict. It was evident that the enemy must be driven from the plain to his stronghold on the heights, and these heights must be stormed. The forces were disposed

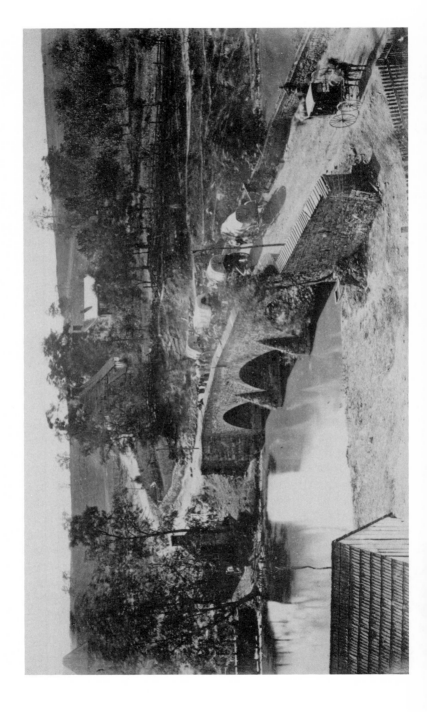

in order of battle before the mists of morning had been dispersed by the rising sun. Our brigade, now commanded by Colonel Rogers, of the Twenty-first New York Vol., held the extreme left, and had the supreme satisfaction of driving the vanguard of the enemy from that part of the field. Batteries B and L made it decidedly too warm for them.

The fight opened fiercely. The great wave of battle surged across the plain and up the rugged heights, swallowing up in its bloody tide regiments, brigades, divisions of brave and heroic men who went down before that death-storm to bite the dust. Great men, men of promise, the sturdy oaks of society as well as the brushwood, were swept by its fury into a soldier's grave. Fortune seemed to favor us, the rebel lines gave way, and our forces drove them up the slope of the heights. But, an avalanche awaited them. A flame of fire leaped from the now uncovered supports and our columns melted before it like dew before the morning sun. The tide of battle changed and rolled back upon the plain.

It was at this point that Lt. Col. N.M. Crane, as inspector-general of General Reynolds' staff, seeing the Pennsylvania reserves in full retreat, rode up to General Reynolds and said: "See yonder, General! the 'reserves' have broken." "My God! Colonel," said the General, "can't you go and stop them?"

Colonel Crane dashed into the midst of the flying mob and by threats, persuasion, and praise of their former deeds of valor, succeeded in rallying a small battalion of them in the face of the storm of lead that followed them.

It was here, also, that General Reynolds, failing to get immediate support from the right, sent in haste to General Doubleday for a brigade. Colonel Rogers was ordered up, and with cheerfulness and spirit the entire brigade moved forward double quick and in perfect line, though the field was continually raked by cannon-shot. Files of men were swept away without a waver in the lines. The expected support arrived before we reached the ground, and the brigade returned to its post. The day had been almost lost, but the veteran regiments were thrown heavily against the triumphant host and quivering under the awful blow, it was beaten back with equal loss. Night at last approached. The sunset was gorgeously beautiful. Nature seemed to

Opposite: The bridge at Antietam (photograph by Alex Gardner; courtesy Library of Congress).

Lt. Col. Nirom M. Crane, field officer, 23rd New York Vol. Regt. (courtesy Library of Congress).

laugh at the great calamity. Fighting did not cease till late and when at last we thought of sleep, we were kept awake by grape and canister.

Sunday morning dawned bright and beautiful and as calm as though the earth had not groaned and the heavens been rent by a scene of carnage seldom equaled in history. Slight cannonading and skirmishing occupied the day and, as we lay down at night with the sky for our cover, Aurora flung out the grand banner of the heavens, "red, white and blue," bespangled by the everlasting stars. Its beautiful folds floated up and covered one half of the arch. As we gazed upon it with delight, we felt that the national emblem had not been dishonored by act of ours and we worshiped in silence the starry banner.

Another day of anxious expectation, of skirmishing and it became evident that our position was untenable. With mastery skill of plan and execution General Burnside placed his army on the east side of the Rappahannock during the night of the 15th, much to the chagrin and disappointment of the foe.

In this engagement the Twenty-third lost two killed and sixteen wounded. There were instances of especial coolness and courage, but to point out these in a regiment where a want of courage is the exception and not the rule, would be unjust to others. Each man, in whatever capacity, did his duty nobly. You will, of course, guess by this letter that your friend came off whole, not damaged.

Yours
P- S-. (Pound Sterling)

Pound Sterling was the pen name of William Maxson.

> We also give Colonel Hoffman's official report of the battle. A minute account of all that we passed through during the five days occupied in this unsuccessful but eventful advance would fill a volume, so we can only give a brief account. This will, however, serve to bring to the mind of the reader a multitude of incidents not mentioned.—William Maxson

Headquarters 23rd NY Vol.

Pratt's Point, Va.
January 2, 1863

Lt. H.P. Taylor, Lieutenant and Acting Adjutant-General 3rd Brigade, 1st Division. 1st Army Corps.

Sir—

In pursuance of orders, I have the honor to report the part taken by my command in the late action at Fredericksburg, December 12th, 13th, 14th, and 15th, to be as follows:

On the morning of the 11th of December we moved with the brigade from our bivouac near White Oak church, on the Belle Plain road, with the intention, as I supposed, of crossing the Rappahannock. We marched but about one and a half miles when we were halted and remained all that day and night, owing to the difficulty and delay in laying the bridges.

That night (11th) the bridges were completed and at early dawn we moved down to the northern bank of the river, at a point about one and a half miles below Fredericksburg, and near the lower bridges, where we remained while the rest of General Franklin's left grand division were crossing. The morning was very foggy until about noon and we did not cross until about two p.m., we being about the last. Soon after the crossing was effected (which was without interruption), we were massed with other troops of the first division near the residence of Mr. Burnard when the enemy for the first time opened upon us from a battery located on the hill opposite, the first striking and bursting in the ground in the flank of my regiment, wounding one man.

They threw about twelve or fifteen shot and shell with remarkably good range while in this position, which resulted in but trifling damage, owing to the fuses in their shell cut either too short or too long.

We soon moved with the rest of the brigade and division to a point directly in front of said Burnard's house, and deployed our line and stacked arms.

General Smith's corps (6th) was deployed on our right, his line running parallel to the river and fronting southwardly and from the river. The lines of our corps (1st), after the deployment, fronted easterly and down the river, the line running perpendicular to the river, the left resting upon it and the right joining the left of General Smith's line and forming a right angle thereto. In this position we lay behind our stacked arms all night.

The morning of the 13th was also foggy, but the fog lifted early and skirmishing commenced along the line, which grew into a general engagement with artillery and small-arms.

We were moved in close massed columns down the river, under a heavy artillery fire from the enemy's batteries, some one and a half miles, when the enemy was found in our front well posted in plain woods and protected by natural rifle-pits.

They were soon dislodged by our artillery, when we advanced with the rest of our division to within about one mile of Massaponax Creek. This position we held all day amid a most terrible artillery fire. Toward evening the enemy concentrated a very hot artillery fire upon us with the evident intention of turning our flank.

The position was maintained, however, although the brigade on our left, the commander of which misunderstood the order, fell back with his command, skirmishers and all, just before dark, whereas his order directed that he should withdraw his brigade a short distance as soon as the darkness would cover his movement from the view of the enemy, but to leave his skirmishers as they were as pickets. This

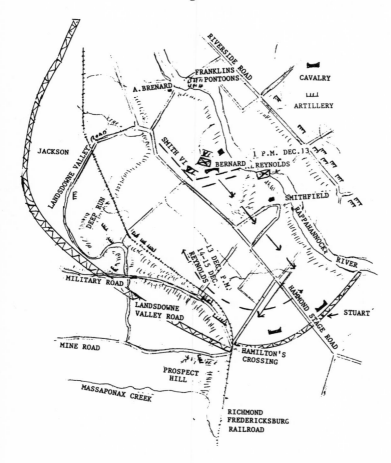

Map showing the Fredericksburg battle area, December 13–15, 1862.

movement being observed by the foe and supposing they had accomplished their design, and that we were falling back, they advanced their line so far that their batteries were within thirty or forty rods of our pickets, and poured a perfect shower of grape promiscuously over the plain until about one hour after dark.

They finally became convinced of their error, ceased firing, and withdrew their lines and all was quiet until morning, except an occasional shot between pickets.

On the 14th and 15th we held the same position without

interruption, except an occasional round from their artillery and sharp picket firing, which was kept up most of the time, day and night, with great briskness.

The picket lines were so close to our advanced position that many of their shots did execution in our ranks.

On the night of the 15th we were withdrawn to the north side of the Rappahannock about midnight, leaving two companies (G and B) on the picket lines not informed (except their commanding officers) that we had retired.

Companies G and B were placed on picket at dusk on the evening of the 15th, and by some misunderstanding or inadvertence on the part of the officer left in charge of the picket, were not informed to retire at the proper time and with the rest of the line, and remained about one hour after the rest had left, and at daylight they fell slowly back, keeping their deployment and stirring up many stragglers and sick who had sought refuge and resting place around the hospital buildings, barns, stacks, river bank, etc., and finally were the last to cross the bridge, it being taken up immediately behind them.

The steadiness and coolness of the officers and men of my command, with very few exceptions, were highly commendable throughout, especially those of Companies A and F, who were on picket during the night of the 14th and during the day of the 15th.

Of the cool and deliberate bravery exhibited by the officers of the two companies G and B under the peculiarly perilous circumstances in which they found themselves, I cannot in justice speak but in terms of especial commendation.

In the action we had engaged one field officer, one acting staff officer (adjutant), fourteen line officers and nine (9) companies, embracing 276 enlisted men.

Company C was detached. We took three (3) prisoners. We had three (3) stragglers.

H. C. Hoffman,
Colonel Commanding

Winter Quarters 1862

The 23rd regiment settled down in a deep ravine six miles below Belle Plains for the winter months. Until such time that the regiment had cleaned out the area from trees and scrub it was nothing but one tangled mess. Soon the oak, pine and greenbrier and what not gave way to a rude but graceful little village.

The campaign that started in March at Fairfax Court House ended after the battle of Fredericksburg at Belle Plain. From late December on, it was nothing but routine camp—drills and picket duty always in the making. In the quiet of the camp, however, the men did find time for fishing which became a great diversion for the soldiers.

Other than Col. H.C. Hoffman's regular official reports to his superiors he took the liberty of writing to a couple of his friends, giving them his own version unofficially of the battle of Fredericksburg.

Dear Major [Gregg] and Dear Thurston:

Gentlemen—your twin letters, dated 18th and 19th of December, were received some days since. I need not say that I was glad to hear from you both. I beg to urge, as an apology for my long delay in answering, and also for writing a co-partnership letter, the fact of my not being in very good health since a few days after the "butchering," and owing to my having a very large amount of official writing to do, which I have not yet finished. General Wadsworth now has command of this (1st) division and General Doubleday has resumed command of his old brigade. Our present position is on the extreme left of the army, we being the last regiment, and resting on the river, as you see by the heading of this, at Pratt's Point or Landing, which is near to and a little below Belle Plain, on the bay that puts up from the Potomac River and into which empties the Potomac Creek.

It is the roughest region just about here that I have seen in Virginia. There is not a level spot close along the river large enough to lie down upon for the night. We are, however, after much hard labor, very comfortably situated, being quartered on the south slope of a hill, with water and wood both convenient and abundant.

We have gone into winter quarters for the third time, and are all well-fixed for the blast. I have a nice fireplace in my tent and am, in every way, prepared to withstand the roughest of weather, provided we remain quiet; but orders have been received which indicate a hurried breaking up again, and probably another fight soon, as our orders read, "Be ready to move at twelve hours' notice, with sixty rounds of cartridges per man and three days' cooked rations on the men, six or eight more in the wagons and cattle enough to last ten days." What the nature of the movement is to be, of course, I do not know, nor do I inquire. It sets prophets and rumor to work and some have it that we are going to the Peninsula and some that we are going back to Washington. Some one thing and some another; but, of course, nothing is so ridiculous but finds credence and publishers. I imagine we are going to attempt the crossing of the Rappahannock at some point above Falmouth and attack the enemy on the flank, or compel him to change front, or else to conform to some movement of his on our right. Whatever it is, I hope that we will meet better success than we did in our last effort. I earnestly wish McClellan had to lead us. I should have more confidence; yet, I do not despair of Burnside, although his last operation was an unfortunate affair. The opinion here was general, that Burnside crossed and fought the late battle in pursuance of positive orders, and against his own wish and judgment; but his manly and self-sacrificing letter to General Halleck, together with his evidence given before the investigating committee, undeceives us on that point and compels us to think even more than ever we did of General Burnside as a high-toned, honorable man, but less as a general.

His original plan was undoubtedly a good one, and had the pontoons arrived at Falmouth with the head of the column, as was expected and doubtless promised, his undertaking would have proved successful beyond a doubt, and long ere this he would have gained a great advantage over the enemy, and made some progress toward Richmond. But the bridges not being there and failing to arrive until after the rebels had seen his design, and before his eyes had prepared for him by erecting strong works on bluffs which are so strong by nature as to be almost impregnable, and massing their entire army behind them, it was in my judgment almost unpardonable in him to lead his army into the face of such a volcano of destruction, merely to appease the craving clamor of some fireside newspaper patriots of the North, for I fail to see how he could hardly hope for a victory.

It would be idle for me to attempt a detailed description of the "butchering" with the few words I could employ for the purpose;

besides, you have doubtless read all the different accounts in the papers, and as far as that goes know more about it than myself, for I have read none of them. In fact, it is an unpleasant theme for me, for you know when a fellow has a fight and got whipped, he is like the boy the calf ran over, "Haint nothing to say," and is not very fond of relating the particulars how it occurred. The whole of it is told, when I say that much the largest, if not the best army that has gone into battle on our side during this war, marched over the river and paraded and drilled around on that beautiful plain for three days and three nights for the butternut cusses to shoot at, until they were satisfied and seemed to have killed all they wanted to, when we sneaked back in the night to this side of the river again.

I knew the lay of the ground over there as well as I do that around Elmira; and so do you Major, if you remember, for our camp last summer, in its different locations, covered almost the entire battle field and knowing it so well I was among the last to believe that we were to cross over at the point we did. It looked to me like a hazardous undertaking—one which any schoolboy who had never heard of battles, after viewing the ground from this side of the Rappahannock, could have advised General Burnside of the fallacy of attempting. You see that I, like all others, grow wonderfully wise and sagacious after the battle is over but let me say that my opinion was expressed and recorded as soon as I knew of the crossing, and long anterior to the battle. On Friday morning early all of General Franklin's grand division was closely packed in the fog on the flats this side of the river previous to and pending the crossing, we being the last to cross, remaining on this side until about one p.m. I had an opportunity of seeing and talking with a great many officers; those with whom I spoke were almost all unanimous in the opinion that the enemy had left or were leaving, from the fact of their offering no resistance to our passage of the stream, for not a gun was fired and it was as still as death. I insisted that unless there was some strong movement being made from some other point and of so formidable a character as to endanger their national capitol (and I had no idea there was, although the rumor was current and by many believed, that Fort Darling had fallen, and that a force of 80,000 was approaching Richmond from Suffolk, etc.), that they were not fools enough to fall back, as their present position was the strongest national defense they had this side of their elaborate fortifications around and in front of Richmond, and that if they dare not fight us where they were they could not afford to anywhere and that I knew the ground and position in which they and we would be in, and gave it as my opinion that they felt secure and confident of holding their ground, as they had a right to do, and that they were no less anxious that we should effect the crossing than we were ourselves, knowing that we would be upon a dead-level plain, without a particle of cover or protection and every man exposed and in range of their most distant guns.

We effected the crossing, the last of us getting over about two p.m. Sure enough, so reliant were they, that when our skirmishers were sent out to feel their position, they never fired a shot, but allowed them to come up close to them, even to conversational distance, told them (the skirmishers)to take their time and get fixed just as they wanted to, and says one of them, "TOMORROW WE WILL DRIVE YOU INTO THE RAPPAHANNOCK, OR YOU WILL DRIVE US INTO HELL." Our lines were formed without interruption.

Notwithstanding all this disadvantage under which I felt we were laboring, I still felt that we were to be successful, for we had the numbers well-equipped and provided for, and then the very desperateness of the undertaking led me to suppose the battle was to be fought on desperate principles. I do not think the battle was planned or fought right. I think, as you sometimes, Major, day, "WEST POINT DEFEATED US," or rather stood in the way of success. The battle was undertaken to be fought on those scientific principles which are supposed to be adopted when you are on something near equal terms with your enemy in numbers and advantage of position. It was undertaken on the same principles of attack that Antietam and other engagements have been fought, and as I think most battles should be fought; but soldier, like experts in any other profession, should be able to govern his actions by circumstances and his surroundings. In the position in which we found the enemy ourselves on the field of Fredericksburg, I believe the plan should have been (if we had not time or inclination to lay a siege), and what I supposed would be done, was to have formed our lines, under cover of the night, close up to our picket line (which was well advanced), in two or three close-sustaining lines of battle, according to the number of men, with the remaining troops in reserve and massed on the flank and center, with the artillery concentrated at each of the different points where they could advance with the line, and at a given signal at day-dawn, with fixed bayonets, let the entire army loose like an avalanche upon their works, making our superior numbers, if we had them, tell upon them. I do not think there should have been a gun loaded until the crest had been carried, but let the men understand that they had the cold steel alone to rely upon, and they would have WENT IN. A man with a load in his gun is very apt to want to stop and go to shooting whenever he is fired upon; whereas, every time he stopped to shoot, at Fredericksburg, the enemy had five-fold the advantage of him, he being entrenched, and the other in an open plain. I am of the opinion, had this been adopted, it would almost certainly have won; we would have stood five chances out of six of defeating them in toto. True, it would have been running this haz-ard—it would have entirely ruined our army or the other; either they would have been demolished or we, ourselves, annihilated. But I sup-posed that was the plan, to end this war before the first of January. I never dreaded going into battle so much as I did crossing that stream; but as soon as across I never was so willing to fight. I had no desire to come back until there had been a complete and decisive victory for one side or the other. I wanted the fighting ended on the spot, so far as these two armies were concerned, and with all my dread of battles, was anxious to run my share of the risk.

The way the battle was fought—by sending one column of attack at this point and another at that to receive the enemy's fire when at a given point from in front and an enfilading fire from both flanks, their artillery in entrenched works and their infantry in rifle-pits sweeping our columns down like grass before the scythe—was very wrong. In this manner of attacking them they would have used up, in my opin-ion, an army of 400,000 men before we could have taken their works. It was the greatest scathing this army ever has taken, and the greatest wonderment to me is that so many escaped unharmed. We had to lay and take it. There was nothing made by dodging, for their guns cov-ered the whole plain on which we stood, and we covered the entire area; so that all they had to do was to shut their eyes and fire, for no shot could fall in the valley without doing execution. They could do as well in the night as in the daytime; and did Saturday night on the extreme left, where old Stonewall sowed grape-shot broadcast over the plain until some time after dark, as lamented old cook used to say when a scratch was made, "HE CAN HIT THEM AS WELL WHERE THEY HAINT AS WHERE THEY ARE." There was a perfect shower of solid shot, shell grapeshot, shrapnel, log-chains and railroad ties all Saturday afternoon.

It is remarkable how polite and respectful this soldiering makes a man. Now both of you know that I am naturally modest, not at all forward in any manners, and am not given to make much of a splurge upon strangers, yet when one of those whizzing cannon-balls came along, I seemed to owe to it that supreme respect, although it being an entire stranger to me, if it comes in recognizing distance, I inadvertently but respectfully bow to it. This seems to be a lesson in etiquette that all easily learn.

I hope General Burnside will not suffer materially by my severe criticism upon his conduct of the late engagement. If he feels bad, I will give him a written certificate that, "with all his mishaps, I love him still." I think very highly of him as a gentleman and an officer, and had rather trust him yet than any in the Army of the Potomac. He is my favorite. He failed once, as the best will. If he leaves, Summer is my next choice. I shall be happy to get and shall accept an answer from you gentlemen, either severally or jointly, or both.

I am, gentlemen, yours truly,
H.C. Hoffman.

Winter Quarters: 1862–1863

Winter Quarters, Va.
Dec. 25, 1862

(Posted Dec. 30, Washington, D.C.)
Friend Ellie:

I should have written to you immediately after the battle of Fredericksburg, had I found a good opportunity for doing so, but since we stuck our tents at Brooks Station before the battle until the present time we have either been moving or placed under circumstances where it was almost impossible to write.

Upon that terrible and disastrous day at Fredericksburg "our boys" all came out again unscathed, although our company suffered quite heavily, losing in killed and wounded one-sixth of our men. It almost seems as though there was a shield around about us. We feel that it is through no goodness of ours that we have thus been spared, but rather a prayer of faith that has ascended to the throne of mercy, from friends at home. Since the battle we have been moving about from one place to another until we finally settled down, it is thought for the winter quarters near Pratts Landing. It is situated a short distance below Bells Landing on the bank of a small bay that pass the waters of the Potomac Creek into the river. It is a pleasant spot for winter quarters. The broad waters of the Potomac are in plain view. The high hills crowned with heavy forests protect us from the chilly winds. The past three days we have been busily engaged in erecting our cabins. We have them, as yet, partially completed. Yet, in this unfinished state one of them seems royal after living in the open December air for a long time. We believe that winter campaigning is at an end. The great conflict which two weeks ago this night hung so imminently over us, and which all were glad to see approaching, has passed. It is now become history. Its managers are laid open to a most jealous people for criticism and condemnation.

Before the appearance of Gen. Burnside's letter to Halleck the army were slow to charge him with the responsibility of the disaster, but there is no longer any room for doubt and with one accord the army cannot do otherwise than charge Burnside with incompetence for the position he holds.

The spirits of the fallen at Fredericksburg must ever rise up in judgment to declare him such, it has only heightened if that could be our former confidence in McClellan. Give us back our "Little Mac" is the united sentiment of this army. There! I have almost forgotten to wish you a "Merry Christmas."

The day has been spent working in the woods on our cabin. Tonight I am sitting here on my boughs of cedar with a pitch fire blazing bright and cheery in our model fireplace, while out of doors the south wind moans through the evergreen boughs of the lofty pines that seem to stand guard over our camp. It almost makes my heart sick when I remember that thousands of America's noblest sons who welcomed the light of this festival one year ago now know it no more upon the earth. They have fallen a sacrifice, but a sacrifice for what ? Has it been for our beloved country or has it been to feed the jealousies and pamper the ambition of unprincipled and unqualified leaders ? It seems hard to decide and was it not for faith that truth and justice shall ultimately prevail. I should, at times, think our cause a hopeless one but the light from the last pitch pine stick is growing dim, I must close.

Merry Christmas
Your true friend
Seymour Dexter

Belle Landing, Va.
Feb. 15, 1863

Dear Friend:

It has been a rainy, gloomy, disagreeable day but as the sun went down the clouds broke and rolled away from before his parting rays, when intervening hills shut them out he decorated the western horizon with a band of gold. Now, as the gentle zephyr blows across the bay it seems like spring. The song of the bluebird and robin now and then greets our ears. We are still acting as provost guard with a good prospect of continuing to do so during the remainder of our time. Nothing worthy of special note has taken place for some time to break the monotony attendant upon the daily routine of our duties. A little excitement, now and then, raised in the arresting of some disorderly soldier or civilian or in the confiscation of subtler goods, which are contraband from the nature of liquors or have been landed contrary to regulations. Not long ago a cargo was such treated. The cause—she pretended to be loaded with apples but a good share of her apple barrels proved to be whiskey barrels, the liquor being put up in bottles and then packed with sawdust in the rough. Such is one of the devices for smuggling the most powerful demoralizers to an army.

The army continues to be literally stuck in the mud. Government teams that came here after supplies appear very much as though the "Sacred Soil" still had a mortgage upon them and was about to close it. In fact, I saw it closed upon one mule team this afternoon to such a degree they were obliged to hitch another team to the mules to get them out of the mire, say nothing about the wagon which stands there yet. Until this mud dries up Hooker will be obliged to remain inactive. No matter what he desires to do or what he is capable of doing, Hooker has been one of the best sub-Generals in the army, but that is not positive proof that he will be the best leader, but I pray God he may prove to be such. When a battle is once opened he will fight with desperation, like Rosecrans at Murfreesboro, he will not retire until he is whipped. When Burnside asked to be relieved if they would have reinstated Gen. McClellan the morale of this army would have went up fifty percent. Troops have been shipping from here for sometime. The PA Res. Div. in which the Bucktails belong have gone to Washington Dept. to reorganize and recruit their decimated ranks. All the artillery and baggage trains belonging to the 9th army corps shipped from here. It is supposed that their destination is No. Carolina. Guard duty is not as severe as before and the rations are improved considerable.

As ever your friend
Seymour

Pratts Landing, Va.
March 9, 1863

(Mailed in Washington D.C. March 11, 1863)
My Dear Friend:

The weather at last is so beautiful that one cannot help being happy. The songs of the birds and the mild breeze bring cheer to the soul as well as to nature. From a neighboring tent comes the sound of Tommy's flute playing while the others are singing some old church pieces from the jubilee. What sweet remembrances seem to come floating along with the familiar strains. I always was an ardent lover of good music but it seems to me that it has grown upon me since I have been a soldier. Perhaps it's because of the lack of it that I appreciate it more.

Last night we had some spring rain but the sun is fast taking away all signs of the rain. It looks now like, from all appearances, it may be some time before Gen. Hooker can move. One year ago tomorrow McClellan began his march up Manassas but there we had good pikes to move upon where here we have nothing of the kind. There is nothing, in fact, at present which indicates an immediate advance. But they are still continuing to give furloughs, but our regiment does not get any at present. They have lately been building storehouses here at the landing. Gen. Hooker has undertaken the duties of his office with an energy that seems to be fast gaining esteem and confidence of his troops.

The health of the old ones is the very best, but with the new regiments there is a large amount of sickness. Hardly a day passes but what we hear the death march played as some deceased soldier is being carried down to the boat to be sent home. Many times there are three or four at the same time. The funeral procession of a soldier is a sad sight, one which I, at least, feel the bitterness of war above all others. Let me die in the strife, confusion and excitement of battle and then thrown into the promiscuous trench rather than linger along in a hospital.

As to taking up my studies when I return where I left them two years ago, I now feel that I could do it and I know there is no stronger inclination in my mind than to do it. But outside influences seem now to be arranging themselves about me so as to deny me the privilege of carrying out my cherished plan of two years. It seems to me now that my school days were past, except next fall and a portion of the winter. Although it is against my inclinations and I believe my adaptation to settle down at home, still my parents cherish plans and their petitions force me, as an only son, to do so.

As ever,
Seymour

Seymour did not mention the fact that he became a corporal on March 1, 1863.

Pratts Landing, Va.
April 7, 1863

Dear Friend:

This is the first I have had a chance in the past several weeks to write. Like N.Y. we have had very little pleasant weather the past month for this climate. Every third day or so usually brings rain or snow and whenever the wind blows from the north it feels as though it just came from the vicinity of a snow bank. Now and then we have one of those beautiful spring days which not only makes all nature smile but seems to radiate joy to all animate beings. The past week we have been expecting the enemy to move. It is reported that Gen. Hooker is sick, hence the delay. A grand review came off yesterday near Falsmouth at which the President was present and I judge he was from the number of salutes fired. There seems to be an entire confidence in the army that we shall be victors in the next engagement. Never was the Army of the Potomac so great a conservator of power as at present. I suppose the defenders of McClellan will be obliged to keep silence since the report of the conduct of the war has made its appearance. Therefore, I take a back seat and keep still. When the army advances, our brigade has been assigned the duty of guarding Aquia Landing and the Railroad with the bridges as far as the Potomac Creek.

Fortifications have been built commanding the bridges, within these the men doing duty will be camped. All the landings here at Belles Plains are to be abandoned.

Although a court of inquiry has exonerated Pope from all blame sustained in the retreat from the Rappadan, yet I am fearful that an impartial court would not do hardly as well. I am counting the days when I will be out.

With that I'll halt.

Seymour

This was the last letter written from the front. On May 11, 1863, the 23rd Regiment embarked on U.S. Mail Steamer John Brooks at Aquia for a trip up the Potomac River to Washington, D.C., where they entrained for home. They left behind part of their lives to bleach in the Virginia soil and the memories of departed comrades-in-arms.

At the old barracks in Elmira, the regiment was cordially received by the Ladies of Elmira with a grand reception that did Elmira proud.

Thus ended the saga of the K Company, 23rd Regiment. The boys from Alfred were mustered out on Wednesday, May 13, 1863.

Epilogue

Independence, N.Y., July 21, 1863

Since his discharge from the army, Seymour found that his time was taken up between lectures, reading and writing, to say nothing of the fact that he had had to turn to on the farm and lend a hand in the necessary chores of farm life. Apparently his lectures on the needs at the front in Virginia had been attended to by the neighboring farmhands, who felt that it was their duty to leave the farms and enlist in the army. Needless to say, Seymour's father's farm suffered as a result; nevertheless, the summer was well spent on the farm. His time away from reading and work was spent lecturing in favor of Abraham Lincoln and the Union.

Long rests and sleep came easily to a young, growing man who had, for many months, been denied these little pleasures of life. He also found time to return to Alfred University's graduation exercises to see some of his old friends.

Seymour confessed that he was glad to be away from the front and the abhorrence of the war in the South, and he felt that his speaking engagements helped salve his conscience. He was quite upset over the riots in New York City and the effect they had had upon the country. He affirmed that it was a dark hour, indeed, for America but not for the brilliant and fruitful victories which had so richly crowned the efforts of the Union armies.

He spent much time and effort to organize Union Leagues. The decision to go back to school was postponed as he had not really made up his mind what he wanted to do. In spite of all of the activities that he was engaged in, his mind continued to be alert. He noted that lonesomeness was not one of his problems.

During the period of time that Seymour was mustered out from the army, many letters that were written were apparently destroyed by his daughter Adelaide, who felt that the contents of the letters were of no apparent value to anyone and she felt that it was her father's wish that the confidences between Seymour and Eleanor remain sacrosanct.

One of the few letters that remains is one that he wrote in October 1863 from Alfred University. He was back in school, apparently having decided to let his heart rule his head, and he had resumed studies. Seymour was delighted to be back in school and wondered why school days could not last forever.

La Sagesse Soutient L'Univers.

FIFTH ANNIVERSARY SESSION
OF
The Athenaeum Lyceum
OF ALFRED UNIVERSITY,
Tuesday morning, June 30th, 1863.

PRAYER.................... ....By. E. E. Kenyon, A. M.
MUSIC—"Hebrew Morning Hymn."
1. CALLING ROLL................ ....Responding by Sentiment.
2. SALUTATORY—"Jessie Benton Fremont,"...Mira Davis, Greenwood.
MUSIC—"The Old College Bell,"
3. ESSAY — { "The Fitness Seen of } ...Ervilla Goodrich, Hornellsville.
        { Sight and Faith," }
4. RECITATION—"Dawn of Redemption,".....Ellen Monahan, Alfred.
5. ORATION — { "The Women of the } ...Clara Banks, Pine Valley.
        { Revolution." }
MUSIC—"Let Me In."
6. PAPER—"Athenæum Tablet,"......Gertrude H. Davis, Greenwood.
7. COLLOQUY...:............... { Emily Hulbert, Canaseraga.
                              { Fauny Sheppard, Alfred.
                              { Mina Sherman, "
                              { Fanny Taylor, Canaseraga.
                              { Nannie Spencer, Alfred.
                              { Nettie Fulmer, Independence.
MUSIC—"Some Things Love Me.
8. POEM — { "The Ruined and the } ....L. S. Bridgeman, Belfast.
        { Rising City. }
9. VALEDICTORY—"Hereafter,"........L. Ettie Livermore, Alfred.
MUSIC—"Fremont's Battle Hymn."
ADJOURNMENT.

Graduation program, Alfred University, June 30, 1863 (courtesy Alfred University Archives).

Seymour Dexter, attorney, 1867 (photograph from collection of Carl Morrell).

At long last, Seymour completed his courses at Alfred University in the spring of 1864, having taken a course in classics that equipped him to study law. He again returned to Elmira and entered the law offices of James Woods to further his education with some practical application. It was under the guardianship of James Woods and the financial assistance from his father, who sent him monthly stipends, that helped him complete his law education.

Elmira, NY
Nov. 3rd, 1864

Dearest Ella:

The fates still wind off from their wheel of fortune that which is favorable to me. Yes, your dear, good, devoted letter found me in the best of spirits. I am happy tonight. I am in the office writing with a flurry of conversation around me. Now, for a full explanation of the "Shade of Sorrow." Some time since I wrote home for some money, father sent it to me by return mail but in the letter he chided me for spending so much money and desiring me to make my education available as soon as possible—and some other things of the same nature.

As it looked in black and white it touched my independence too much to stand. I sat down and wrote a long letter answering, in which I told him I did not desire him to send me money if it made him feel as the letter seemed to represent. If he could not send me money without writing such sentiments, to stop it and say so.

I began to think that he had concluded to let me see what I could do for myself. I got tired of waiting for an answer and wrote for a decision. I received a very good letter in reply and he sent me some more money, saying that he intended to furnish me money to the amount he had promised. Hence, the shades of sorrow are all removed and my usual good spirits prevail and after your good letter how could I be otherwise? I confess that I would like to sit down by your side and feel your cheek against mine and your arm around my neck. No, I don't think my Ella foolish. I have been making some appearances since I last wrote.

I like Turner. He offered to lend me money to continue right along in the office if I did not get it from home. I am going to Independence tomorrow as I speak at Whitsville tomorrow evening and at Hallsport the next night. As for Monday night no appointments have been given out but I shall speak for "Honest Abe."

I am alone in the office now and how I do wish I were going to meet you when I leave. It is now simply a wish, but if fates continue to smile it shall be realized in the future. I love this quiet because I can think of you. I know you will be happy when you read this, happy because I am happy. May God bless and protect you. Goodnight with a kiss.

Your devoted Seymour

Ellenoir Weaver Dexter, late 1860s (photograph from collection of Carl Morrell).

It can be noted at this time that the letter salutations to Ellie from Seymour have changed from "Friend" and "Classmate" to "Dear" and "Dearest Ellie."

It was in the Woods office on the eve of December 31, 1864, that Seymour first sent his proposal of marriage to Ellie. Knowing that bar examinations were yet two years away, he felt that marriage was just as far away and would not consider entering into matrimony until the time came that he had passed his bars, to say nothing of the fact that his father had promised him financial aid until that time and no longer.

Elmira
December 30, 1864

Dearest Ella,

'Tis Friday evening. Woods & Turner have both gone out calling, leaving me all "alone in my glory," so now for an answer to your last good letter. I don't mean to be obliged to wait two weeks this time for another. I intended to answer last evening but Frank Mason offered me a ticket and wanted me to attend a concert with him held at Elys hall. There was a fine display of art in both the instrumental and vocal fields and we were certainly charmed by the singing. It was the best we had heard in some time.

I have had several pressing social engagements but the pressure of the office has me on the run at this time, later perhaps, now I cannot afford the time to play much. I feel contented and happy in this laboring while I feel that I am being successful and I know that you are happy. The blues is something that does not trouble me often. I hope now that when I write you again I shall be so situated that I can tell father that I don't need his assistance any longer although it will retard my study of law, yet I shall feel better and I believe you will like it also.

I desire now, my Jewel, to be so situated that I may call you mine by a legal title two years from New Years Eve. What say you to the time ????

Sad, indeed, the story you write of Mrs. Babcock but in these days of ours our ears have become accustomed to stories of bloodshed and carnage, our eyes so accustomed to see some of the results that such scenes do not fill us with horrors as of old. We, as a people, value not human life today as we did four years ago.

With the advent of real cold weather I have spent much of my leisure time (what I can find of it) on the ice skating rink. You must learn to skate as we will be doing a lot of it. I also spent the later hours with Tennyson. I weigh now more than ever before and increasing, certainly it's not from grief.

Since you will not receive this until 1865, I wish you a "Happy New Year" with the hope of bringing you a happier one in the future. Remember me to your parents.

Yours as ever
Seymour

At long last the studies were completed and Seymour passed his bar exams in Binghamton in May 1866, and was admitted to the fraternity of lawyers. In the following years he joined the George M. Diven law firm as a managing clerk. In 1868 he formed a partnership with Robert Turner and E. C. Van Duzer, who also joined the firm at the same time. It was during this partnership that Seymour and Ellenoir Weaver became married, as he had promised in his letter of December 1864. On June 17, 1868, their pact was consummated and they became husband and wife, settled down and, as it were, "lived happily ever after." Their marriage was blessed with six children: Daniel, Luin, Emily, Adelaide, Eleanor and Mary.

In the spring of 1872 Judge Dexter was appointed city attorney and in the fall of 1872 he was elected to the State Assembly, being the first Republican elected to that office in 17 years. He declined an offer of unanimous renomination and in 1877 was elected county judge and surrogate on the GOP ticket.

In 1875 Seymour Dexter organized the Chemung Valley Savings and Loan Association and became its first president, a position he held until his demise. He also started an organization of the New York State League of Building and Loan Associations. He became the first president of the United States League of Building and Loan Associations in 1893. In spite of the demands upon his time he found the time to write and lecture.

Seymour Dexter, among other things, managed to find time to devote his energies to the New York State Reformatory Board of Directors and the New York Chamber of Commerce. He was also treasurer and trustee of Elmira College as well as treasurer and director of the State Library Association. He was president of the Elmira Advertiser Association, which formerly owned the Elmira Advertiser.

His position on the New York State Reformatory Board led him into a unique position as teacher. Apparently the penal system in New York, even in those early days, was aware of the need for instruction and rehabilitation of the convicts.

From September 1885 until May 1886, Judge Dexter conducted classes at the Reformatory in political economy. Classes were held every two weeks. His notes from his lectures were published by the New York State Reformatory schools under the title of "The Outline of Political Economy." The subject matter covered taxes and its forms, wealth of the nation, and needs of capital and labor.

He also, at the same time, delivered lectures to church groups and other organizations on "Excessive Productive Energy" entailing the problems of production and distribution of food and commodities.

His ability as an orator, political leader, and civic and social activist won recognition in 1885 and 1903 when Alfred University conferred the degrees of Doctor of Philosophy and the Doctor of Laws upon him.

The partnership of Turner, Dexter & Van Duzer was thereupon dissolved on January 1, 1878. The term of county judge was six years, at the close of which Judge Dexter was re-elected and held the office until August 1889, when he resigned to accept the presidency and active management of the Second National Bank, a position of trust and responsibility which he held until he died in 1904. A banquet was tendered him by the Bar of the County on October 11, 1889, commemorative of his retirement, at which the following resolutions were adopted and other evidences given of the esteem in which he was held by his professional brethren:

When the recognition of a man by his peers results in his selection for prominent positions and the performance of duties requiring unusual qualifications, perfect integrity and an exalted moral character, he has just reason to be proud.

Success in lines chosen at the threshold of life is earnestly desired by every man of healthy brain and body, and nothing is so sweet and satisfying as the realization, in middle life, of his youthful hopes and ambitions.

To have accomplished our ends in life, and to be able to stand on a foundation built by our own hands, firmly embedded in the esteem and unqualified respect of our neighbors and friends, is to have made life worth living.

Uninterrupted advancement toward the goals so inviting to all, and holding them within the grasp, is accorded to few. But to know how others see us is rarely permitted and truthful words of praise from sincere friends are like "apples of gold in pictures of silver." Such has been your career and rewards since you became a member of this bar.

For the past decade your judicial life on the bench of this

Seymour Dexter, 1904 (photograph from collection of Carl Morrell).

county has been so characterized by impartiality, varied learning, integrity, and unvarying regard for professional ethics as to justly entitle you to the lasting respect of this community.

While deeply regretting your retirement from the practice of our profession, we heartily wish for you and yours a continuance of success in the new walk you have chosen.

In spite of the many tasks and fields of endeavors that he had undertaken, Seymour still found time to remain active in military affairs in a small way. The Southern Tier Rifles reformed in October 1874. They became the 110th Battalion Company D, 20th Brigade, Seventh Division of the National Guard, State of New York. Seymour enrolled at the time as a 2nd lieutenant and remained active with the group until 1877, at which time the 110th Battalion disbanded and re-formed as the 30th Infantry Company Seymour remained active with the 30th until 1896.

Seymour Dexter was indeed a man of boundless energy with a great abundance of faith in his fellow man. He was sincerely dedicated to the causes he felt were right and just. Duty to God, man, and country was indeed of primary importance. He maintained throughout his life at character of spirit and courage that helped shape the course and destinies of this nation.

After a lingering illness, Seymour Dexter passed away on May 5, 1904. His death brought expressions of sorrow from men and organizations all over the nation. The Elmira Advertiser *aptly eulogized: "He was a well-rounded man in all those attributes which make for nobility of soul, staunchness of character and breath of intellectual development."*

Appendix A:
Field and Staff of the 23rd N.Y. Volunteer Regiment

MAY 16, 1861

HENRY C. HOFFMAN	Colonel, commissioned May 16, 1861
NIROM M. CRANE	Lt. Colonel, commissioned May 16, 1861
WILLIAM M. GREGG	Major, commissioned May 16, 1861
MYRON H. MANDEVILLE	Quartermaster, with rank of 1st Lieutenant
WILLIAM W. HOYT	Adjutant, with rank of 1st Lieutenant
SEYMOUR CHURCHILL	Surgeon, with rank of Major
WILLIAM A. MADILL	Assistant Surgeon, with rank of 1st Lieutenant
EZRA CRANE	Chaplain
ARCHIBALD N. DEVOE	Sergeant Major
HIRAM SMITH	Quartermaster Sergeant
MILES TERRILL	Drum Major
JULIUS C. SMEAD	Fife Major
JAMES DEBOIS	Appt. Chaplain in place of Ezra Crane who resigned January 26, 1862
THOMAS H. STILLWELL	Assistant Surgeon
WILLIAM TAYLOR	Assistant Surgeon

Appendix B: Original Roll of Company K (and Changes Made During Two Years of Service)

ORIGINAL STAFF

1. NATHANIEL B. FOWLER: Captain, Commissioned May 6, 1861.

2. FLORENCE SULLIVAN: 1st Lieutenant, Commissioned May 16, 1861. Resigned February, 1863.

3. RODNEY W. STEELE: 2nd Lieutenant, Commissioned May 1, 1861. Died of remittent fever Dec. 7th, 1861, while on leave in Elmira, N.Y., in his home.

4. DUANE THOMPSON: 1st Sergeant, Appointed May 16, 1861. Promoted to 2nd Lt. Jan. 25, 1862, to fill the vacancy made by death of Rodney Steele. Again promoted to 1st Lt. March 1, 1863, to fill vacancy of Florence Sullivan who resigned.

5. ISREAL REYNOLDS: 2nd Sergeant, appointed May 16, 1861. Discharged Jan 12, 1863, for disability.

6. LUCIUS W. BINGHAM: 3rd Sergeant, appointed May 16, 1861. Promoted Commissary Sergeant Aug. 1, 1861. Again promoted to Quartermaster, with rank of 1st Lieutenant Dec. 22, 1862.

7. JUDD D. BURT: 4th Sergeant, appointed May 16, 1861. Promoted to 1st Sergeant Jan. 25, 1862. Appointed 2nd Lt. March 1, 1863, to fill vacancy of Duane Thompson.

8. JOSEPH M. ROE: 1st Corporal, appointed May 16, 1861. Has been in hospital since Oct. 1, 1862.

9. GEORGE N. CLATE: 2nd Corporal, appointed May 16, 1861. Promoted to Sgt. Jan 1, 1862. Promoted to 1st Sgt. March 1, 1863, in place of Judd Burt who was promoted.

10. THADDEUS A. COWEN: 3rd Corporal, appointed May 16, 1861. Promoted to Sgt. Aug. 1, 1861. Discharged for disability Nov. 26, 1862.

11. LORENZO HOWES: 4th Corporal, appointed May 16, 1861. Taken prisoner at battle of Bull Run on night of Aug. 29, 1862. Exchanged and returned to Regt. Oct. 20, 1862. Since, he acted as Brigade Commissary Clerk.

JUNIOR OFFICERS

1. CHRISTOPHER C. ATKINS

2. *LUCIOUS BACON: Died of remittant fever Sept. 6, 1861 at Columbia College Hospital. Buried at the Soldier's Home.

3. DANIEL G. BECKWITH: Wounded at battle of Fredericksburg, Dec. 13, 1862. Left leg taken off by cannon shot.

4. WILLIAM H. BETSON: Appointed corporal March 1, 1863.

5. *WALLACE W. BROWN: Transferred to 1st Regt. Pennsylvania Vol. (Bucktails), promoted to hospital steward.

6. DAVID K. BUNNELL

7. JOHN W. BURKE: Discharged Oct. 1, 1861. Died at his home of consumption.

8. EDMUND CROCKER: Discharged Oct. 2, 1862, for disability.

9. *CHARLES A. CHAPIN: Appointed corporal Aug. 1, 1861. Promoted to sergeant March 1, 1863.

10. HENRY C. COLEMAN: Appointed corporal Aug. 1, 1861. Appointed hospital warden and then promoted to brigade commissary sergeant.

11. STEVEN T. COVELL: Appointed corporal Aug. 1, 1861. Appointed hospital warden and promoted to brigade commissary sergeant.

12. SIMEON COULP

13. I. NEWTON COWEN

14. PATRICK CURTIN

15. *SEYMOUR DEXTER: Slightly wounded in battle of Antietam. Appointed corporal March 1, 1863.

16. GEORGE F. DUDLEY: Discharged for promotion to 1st lieutenant in 103 Regt. N.Y. Vol. on February 22, 1862.

17. HENRY T. DUNN: Discharged Sept. 25, 1861. Appointed midshipman U.S. Naval Academy.

18. LEVI W. ESSLESTINE: Wounded at battle of Antietam in the knee by cannon shot.

19. CHARLES B. ESTEE

20. CHARLES FOSTER: Detached in 1st N.Y. Battery June 10, 1862. Returned to company April 4, 1863.

21. ALONZO D. GRIFFIN: Appointed miltary telegraph operator in July 1861. Died at Fortress Monroe in Feb. 1863.

22. WILLIAM E. GRIFFITHS: Discharged for disability February 4, 1863.

23. DANIEL B. HURLBURT: Discharged for disability June 1, 1862.

24. FREDERICK HAMILTON: Acting drum major of Drum Corps.

*Students from Alfred Academy, Alfred, N.Y.

25. SIMON Q. HOWARD: Musician. Discharged Dec. 4, 1862, for disability.

26. THOMAS HENDERSON: Appointed corporal Aug. 1, 1863. Promoted to sergeant. March 1, 1863.

27. WILLIAM S. JESSUP: Wounded in leg at battle of Fredericksburg Dec. 13, 1862.

28. MILLARD G. JOHNSON: Appointed corporal Feb. 25, 1862.

29. *LOUIS KENYON

30. MICHAEL LEMMON

31. GEORGE E. LEWIS: Appointed corporal March 1, 1862.

32. DAVID LYONS: Discharged May 8, 1862, disability.

33. RICHARD LONG

34. RICHARD LYONS: Discharged July 21, 1862, disability.

35. FRANK H. MANDEVILLE: Appointed brigade forage master.

36. J. EDMUND B. MAXSON: Died in Upton Dale, Va., Feb. 27, 1862, of hemorrhage caused by accidental pistol-shot wound.

37. *WILLIAM P. MAXSON: Author of the "Campfires of the Twenty-Third" under pen name of (P.S.) Pound Sterling.

38. WILLIAM EDGAR MAXSON

39. AUGUSTUS W. MEYERS: In hospital since July 9, 1862.

40. GEORGE W. MEYERS: Discharged July 9, 1862, for disability.

41. JAMES MURTHA

42. IRA N. MCKIBBEN: Appointed corporal Feb. 25, 1862. Promoted to sergeant March 1, 1863.

43. S.G. HATHWAY MUSGRAVE

44. EDMUND B. PICKERING: Discharged Nov. 14, 1861, for disability.

45. JAMES W. PICKERING

46. JOHN L. POOL: Discharged Dec. 21, 1861 for disability.

47. GEORGE W. PARKER

48. HOSEA H. ROCKWELL

49. JAMES R. RATHBONE: Discharged May 4, 1862 for disability.

50. WILLIAM H. ROBINSON: Discharged Jan. 6, 1862 for disability.

51. MARK SHEPARD: Discharged May 15, 1862, for disability.

52. JOHN W. SANDERS

53. *THOMAS C. SANDERS: Detached in 1st N.H. Battery June 26, 1862. Taken prisoner at second battle of Bull Run Aug. 29, 1862. Rejoined the company January 1863.

*Students from Alfred Academy, Alfred, N.Y.

54. GEORGE W. STRATTON: Discharged Sept. 25, 1861, for disability.

55. JAMES SIMMONS: Killed at battle of Fredericksburg by cannon shot Dec. 13, 1862. Buried on the field.

56. MARTIN B. SPAFFORD

57. THOMAS G. STULL

58. LEMUEL B. STOWELL: Has been in General Hospital since July 10, 1862.

59. CHARLES W. SWEET: Taken prisoner at second battle of Bull Run Aug. 30, 1862, while in charge of Lt. Bouvier of General Patrick's staff who was wounded on the night of Aug. 30, 1862. Rejoined the company on Oct. 31, 1862.

60. CHARLES F. STEPHENS: Discharged June 17, 1862, disability.

61. *LUIN K. THATCHER: Discharged March 22, 1862 for promotion to adjutant of 9th Kansas Vol. Cavalry. Subsequently was appointed major.

62. *JOHN C. TODD: Appointed corporal March 1, 1863.

63. WILLIAM B. TORRENCE: In hospital since May 27, 1862.

64. JOSEPH M. UPDEGRAFF: Shot by patrol April 12, 1862 at Bristow, Va. Buried on the 15th.

65. ROBERT B. VANGORDER: Appointed corporal Aug. 1, 1861. Wounded in hand while on picket duty Aug. 14, 1861. Discharged December 29, 1862.

66. WILLIAM M. WALTERS: Discharged Oct. 19, 1862, for disability.

67. *GEORGE A. WILLIAMS: Appointed hospital warden in February 1863.

68. WILLIAM H. HOOD

69. HENRY P. WORMLY

70. NORTHRUP P. YOUNG

RECRUITS

71. DANIEL S. ALLEN

72. CHARLES W. ANDREWS

73. GEORGE BAKER: Detached in Battery L, lst NY Artillery, in Nov. 1862. Returned to company Feb. 8, 1863.

74. STEPHEN T. BAKER: In General Hospital since Oct. 30, 1862.

75. MARVIN BECKWITH: Accidently wounded by a minié ball through the thigh while on picket duty in January 1862.

76. JOHN R. FRANKS

77. PATRICK J. GUINAN: Wounded at Fredericksburg on Dec. 13, 1862, by piece of shell in thigh.

78. MICHAEL GRADY: Taken prisoner at battle of Bull Run on night of Aug. 30, 1862. Returned to company Oct. 31, 1862.

*Students from Alfred Academy, Alfred, N.Y.

79. GEORGE W. HOLBERT: Discharged March 22, 1862, disability.

80. GEORGE W. HENDERSHOT: Discharged Nov. 28, 1862, disability.

81. CLINTON ROBINS: Taken prisoner at battle of Bull Run while in charge of Lt. Bouvier of Gen. Patrick's staff; wounded on night of Aug. 29, 1862. Rejoined the company Oct. 31, 1862. Wounded at battle of Fredericksburg in the leg by piece of shell.

82. JOHN H. HICKS

83. JAIRUS LAMOUREE

84. ALLEN PACKARD

85. JUSTIN R. REAMER

86. EDWARD E. ROCKWELL

87. THOMAS W. OAKLY: Discharged July 11, 1862, for disability.

88. SAMUEL W. SEARLES: Appointed clerk in Carver Hospital in May 1862.

89. CHARLES C. THOMPSON: Appointed corporal March 1, 1863.

90. EMANUEL VANDERMARK: Deserted December 17, 1861.

91. CHARLES W. WEBSTER: Discharged Oct. 19, 1862, on account of injuries received by railroad accident while on his way to the regiment.

Statistical references (appendices A and B) were taken from William Maxson's book Campfires of the 23rd *which was written at the close of the Civil War.*

References

Downey, Fairfax. *The Guns Roll On*. Taken from the *Journal of the Company of Militarian Historians*, spring 1980 (Ref: The First New Hampshire Battery).

History of the 30th. Separate Co. National Guard, N.Y. 1896. Commentary and sketches of National Guard activity from its inception in 1832 until 1896.

Maxson, William. *Campfires of the 23rd*. 1863. A saga of the 23rd N.Y. Vol. Infantry. All battle references by officers were taken from this book.

Towner, Ausbury. *History of Chemung County*. Syracuse, N.Y.: Mason Press, 1892

The Union Army: A History of Military Affairs in the Loyal States, 1861–1865, volumes 2, 5 and 6. Federal Publishing, 1908.

Letters from Col. H.C. Hoffman's private files are used with the permission and courtesy of Mrs. Allyn C. Hoffman, Elmira, N.Y.

Index